HISTORIC QUABBIN HIKES

By J. R. Greene

Printed by Highland Press, Athol, Mass.

ISBN 1-884132-01-4

All illustrations are from the author's collecion, unless otherwise identified.

Front cover illustration shows a bedstead with tree growing through it, formerly near the Katie Whipple cellarhole in Dana, photographed in 1982 by Michael R. Watt.

To Donna

Who has never seen most of these places

CONTENTS

(Chapter numbers in Roman numerals)

PREFACE

The author of this guide has been writing about the Quabbin, and hiking in its watershed since 1975. During this time, in spite of many new books about the human and natural history of the Quabbin, no one had produced a guide-book for the visitor wishing to explore its historic places.

Hopefully, this basic guide to several historic sections of the reservation will fill a need in satisfying the public's curiousity. No attempt will be made here to address the interests of naturalists, bird watchers, geologists, or fishermen; that will have to be undertaken by others.

While large parts of the Quabbin Reservation are closed off to the public (including the islands and Prescott Peninsula), there are still many sites of historic interest that can be hiked or bicycled to. This is especially true of the northern reservation lands, which include the largest acreages between the reservoir and the outer boundaries open to the public.

The careful reader may find that sections of watershed lands on the western and southeastern sides of the reservoir have been excluded from this book. A conscious decision was made to do this, for two reasons. First, because there were no villages of note in these narrow sections (except the two covered) and, secondly, because the fascinating history of the many mills in the eastern Pelham area is well documented in Paul Bigelow's 1993 book *"Wrights and Privileges."* That book is highly recomemnded to those who wish to explore that section.

Extracts from the regulations affecting hikers and bicyclers in the Quabbin Reservation (as this book went to press) are in the appendix. Knowledge of these regulations will enable the law-abiding citizen to visit the accessable parts of the Quabbin without fear of encountering problems. A list of books and pamphlets used as sources for this book, which will further enlighten the reader, is also appended.

The author would like to acknowledge the assistance of the following individuals; M.D.C. Employees Bruce Spencer, Clif Read, Terry Campbell,

David Small, David Supczak, Peter Izyk, and Joseph Burek; also Ruth Bassingthwaite, Paul Bigelow, Les Campbell, Roy Hanks, Hilda (Olafson) Hastings, Marty Howe, Robert Keyes, Janet Kraft, Sam Paoletti (longtime fellow hiker), Kay Reed, Carol (Anderson) Rich, Michael Watt (for his new photos and encouragement), and Aubie Weaver.

Also thanks to the staffs of the following libraries for the use of their materials; Athol, Univ. of Mass., Amherst College, and Jones (all three in Amherst), Woods (Barre), Mass. State Archives (Boston), Forbes (Northampton), Pelham, and the Connecticut Valley Historical Society (Springfield).

Any errors in this book are the responsibility of the author. If any can be documented, please write to him at the address inside the front cover, so that corrections can be made in any future edition.

J. R. Greene
August, 1994

FORMAT OF THIS BOOK

A vast area of the Swift River Valley was covered by the Quabbin Reservoir when it was flooded in the 1940s. Several major village sites, including Enfield, the two Greenwiches, and North Dana were inundated. The site of Prescott Hill village was heavily damaged by the siting of the radio astronomy facility there; it and the site of Atkinson Hollow are within the off-limits sections of the watershed, so they will be excluded from this guide. Nichewaug in Petersham, and Cooleyville in New Salem are both outside of the "general taking line" for the Quabbin, and each still has a few houses within their former limits, so they will also be excluded from consideration here. In spite of these omissions, there are still the sites of two villages and several hamlets above the reservoir flowline that can be explored.

Even with 38.5 square miles of the valley inundated, there are still many remains of the two centuries of human habitation within the Quabbin reservation. The most historically intriguing sections that can be visited by hikers will be noted in succeeding chapters.

A brief history of the reservoir will be presented before the hikes are described, in order to aid the reader in understanding why this place is much different from most bodies of water or public reservations in Massachusetts. More detailed historical material can be found in other publications (including the author's), which are listed in the appendix.

The remaining chapters will describe portions of the watershed that can be hiked over during a single trip. Almost all of the cellarholes along each route will be identified, including the name of the last owner, and some previous ones. References to owners at earlier times are mostly taken from various county atlases (see sources), and from M.D.C. property records. These listings will be convenient for those who have access to the atlases in libraries. Portions of topographic maps will be used to aid the hiker in identifying locations on the ground.

Some buildings and homes will be illustrated, especially those in the Dana Common area. The Water Commission photographed almost all of the properties in the valley, but most of these are very sterile views. For those who wish to look up locations not pictured in this book, prints of the M.D.C. property photos are on file at the Administration Building at Quabbin; the negatives are at the Mass. Archives in Boston. Only a few M.D.C. pictures are reproduced in this book; most of the photos used are from the suthor's collection, except where otherwise credited.

The pictures, and descriptions of some of the places and people who lived there are meant to give greater meaning to what are now just sites or cellarholes, whether you attempt to visit them, or just read about them. Having an illustration of an old home in front of you when you are standing next to the cellarhole can be an enlightening experience.

So, take this book with you on your next trip to the Quabbin, whether it be for a day, or just a quick hike from a parked motor vehicle. Use it to get an idea what the people of the lost valley and their lives were like.

KEY MAP OF QUABBIN RESERVOIR

(Numbers in circles are highways, numbers in squares are M.D.C. gate numbers)

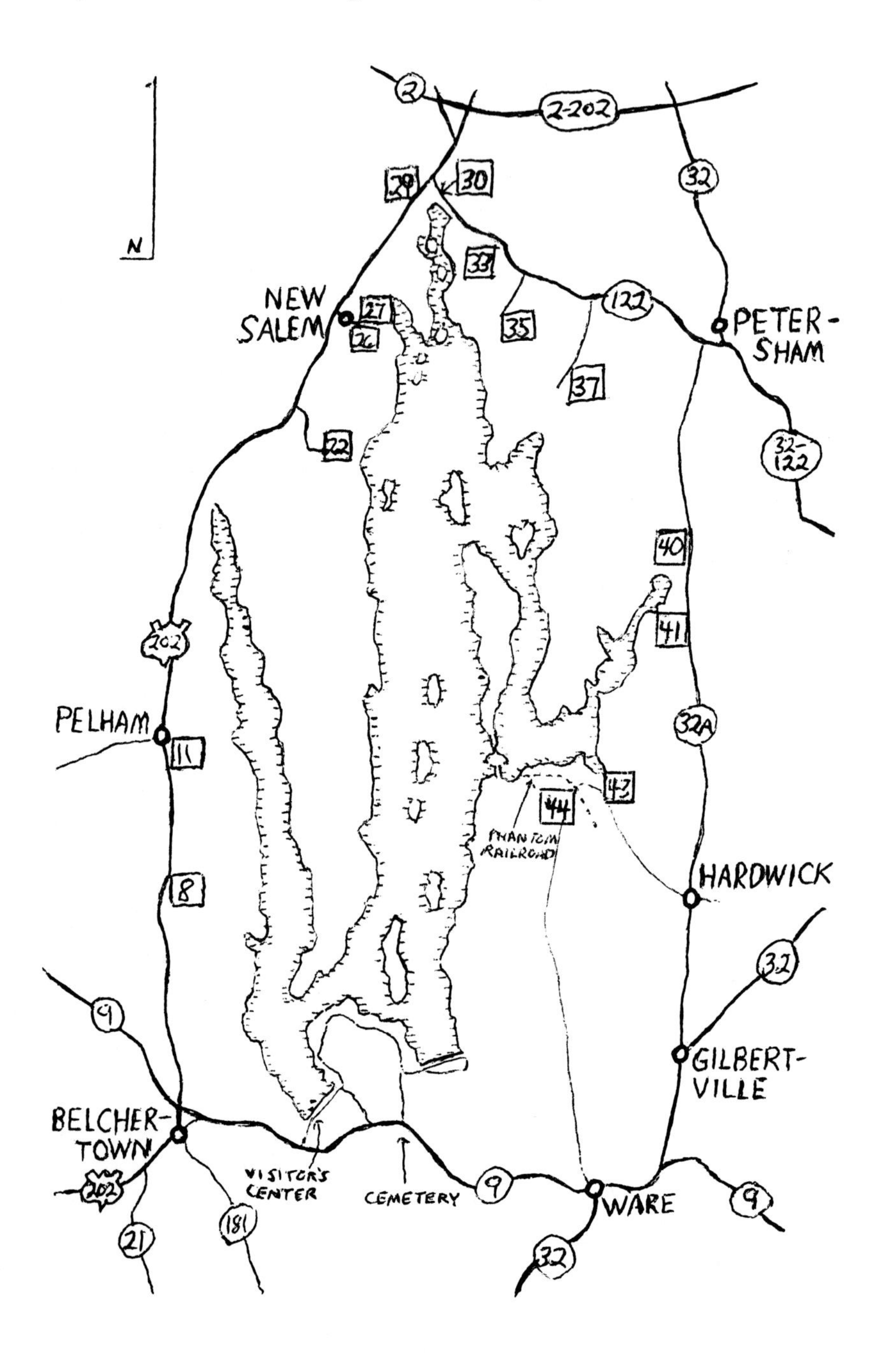

Chapter 1 - ABOUT THE LOST TOWNS

This chapter will provide a few details about the human history of the Swift River valley. For more information, consult the books listed in the appendix.

American Indians inhabited the valley before the arrival of white settlers in the 1730s. Writers differ over whether these Indians were Nipmucs, Pocumtucs, or even Quaboags. The sachem (or chief) of a local tribe was reportedly named Nini- (or Nani-) Quabbin. The word Quabbin itself meant great waters, or well-watered place.

These natives were driven out of the area after the King Phillip War of 1675-6. A few are mentioned as still living in the Swift River valley at the time of white settlement.

There was an impetus to settle the remaining uninhabited lands in Massachusetts east of the Connecticut River in the early 1730s. As a result, Belchertown, Greenwich, New Salem, and Petersham were opened up to white colonists during this decade.

These towns, as originally laid out, were usually larger in extent than their final shape. Because residents of remote parts of town did not want to travel so far for church or town meetings, separate districts or parishes were formed.

The southwestern part of Greenwich formed a separate parish in 1786 (this became Enfield in 1816). In the same year, eastern Pelham formed a parish, which became part of Prescott in 1822. Dana was created out of parts of Petersham, Greenwich, and Hardwick in 1801.

Enfield was the most populous (1,000) and prosperous of the four fated towns. Its farming and industries made it one of the wealthier towns per capita in the state before the Civil War.

Dana also prospered, with industries concentrating in its North village. Greenwich and Prescott were mainly farming communities, and suffered from the decline in New England agriculture after the Civil War.

Ironically, the arrival of the railroad in the valley in 1871 did not spur many new industries, but it did ship in farm products from the west.

Greenwich, Mass., around 1905

This helped drive many valley farmers into raising poultry and livestock, or growing apples and berries to survive. Ice cut from local ponds was shipped out by rail as far away as New York City.

By the early 1900s, many valley ponds began to attract summer camps, both private and institutional. Besides the camps they built, some stayed at local hotels. This became a major factor in the economies of Greenwich and North Dana by World War I.

When the valley was first proposed as a reservoir site in 1895, most prople dismissed the scheme as a fantasy. When the proposals took on a serious note by 1920, the valley was in a vulnerable state. From a peak of 3,453 souls in 1850, the population of the four doomed towns fell to 2,024 in 1920. Only a couple of factories each in North Dana and Enfield were still operating by the early 1920s.

Facing the inevitable, valley residents used their meager resources to fight for fair compensation for their property, rather than oppose the reservoir project itself. It must be noted that various civil rights and environmental organizations that would have pitched in against a project like this in the 1980s and 1990s either did not exist, or were not concerned.

The valley folk did not gain much for their efforts; businesses and employees dislocated by the

Wachusett Reservoir were compensated far more generously than they were.

Landowners within the affected area were sent forms to fill out describing their property. Appraisers hired by the Commission evaluated the real estate. Then an offer was made. If the property owner accepted it, the sum was paid, and the place would be vacated. Some were allowed to rent back their home; or the Commission would rent it to someone else - often a project worker.

Property settlements were not generous, especially during the depths of the Great Depression in the early 1930s. People who could afford lawyers appealed the offers to a board of referees, or brought suit in a land court.

An exodus began in 1927-28, as many wanted to sell out and rebuild their lives as soon as possible. Prescott lost over 3/4 of its inhabitants, which forced the Water Commission to operate that town's functions from 1928 to 1938. However, when it became known that it would take several years to complete the project, the exodus slowed somewhat.

Many people stayed on in the valley as long as they could. Some left when their jobs ceased with the closing of valley businesses and factories. The ending of service on the "Rabbit" railroad in June, 1935 encouraged some to leave.

The population of the four towns fell by about 30% from 1925-1930, but only by about 19% in the following five years. This slowing of the decline may be partly due to the influx of engineers and project workers, many of whom rented homes in the valley.

The only industry to survive the demise of the valley was the Swift River Box Shop in North Dana. It (and several of its employees) moved to Athol in 1935, operating there until the 1950s.

Only a few dozen valley residents' homes were moved or rebuilt elsewhere. Most houses were torn down, burned, or bulldozed into their foundations. A few of the exceptions are noted in Chapter 23. Most of the valley people removed to within 25 miles of the reservoir. The moving experience was not made any easier by a total lack of relocation assistance from the Water Commission or the state.

Graves in valley cemeteries were disinterred and removed. Most were reburied at the new Quabbin Park Cemetery in Ware (see Chapter 5); others were removed to cemeteries chosen by next-of-kin.

By 1938, enough people had left the valley, and the project was so close to completion, that the state passed as act disincorporating the four towns of Dana, Enfield, Greenwich, and Prescott. This event was marked by a Farewell Ball in the Enfield Town Hall on April 27, 1938. Hundreds of people attended, some coming from far away for a last look at the valley and a chance to see old friends.

Local societies, such as Granges and women's clubs, handed in their decades-old charters and disbanded that spring. Grade schools in the valley held their last classes that June, most holding "graduation" ceremonies for the students to remember. That summer, most of the remaining residents and renters moved away, and four of the last five post offices in the valley closed (Enfield's hung on until January, 1939).

Late in 1938, into 1939, the final destruction of the valley towns took place. Buildings that were not moved or purchased for the wood were burned, or bulldozed into their foundations. The only things left standing below the future flow line of the reservoir were stonewalls and roads. By the time the flooding began in August, 1939, two centuries of the white man's presence here was reduced to ruins.

Chapter 2 – A BRIEF HISTORY OF QUABBIN RESERVOIR

The Quabbin Reservoir is the largest body of water in the Metropolitan Boston water supply system. This system began with the City of Boston's drawing water from ponds outside of its limits as early as 1795.

After opening the Lake Cochituate supply in 1848, additions to the system were made to meet water needs. Several small reservoirs were built on the Sudbury River in Framingham and Marlboro in the 1870s and 1880s. From 1895 to 1908, the Wachusett Reservoir was built by damming the Nashua River above Clinton. This project caused the removal of a village and many homes to clear the 6 1/2 square mile area flooded. This was built and run by the Metropolitan Water Board, which served Boston and several suburbs.

By the time the Metropolitan District Commission absorbed the Water Board (in 1919) another study was underway to augment the system. A 1922 report recommemded what was finally enacted after four years of legislative wrangling. This established the Metropolitan District Water Supply Commission (hereinafter the "Water Commission") to build a diversion of the Ware River in Barre, a reservoir in the Swift River Valley, and an aqueduct to connect it all to the Wachusett Reservoir.

This Commission appointed Frank E. Winsor its Chief Engineer late in 1926; he served until his death in 1939. A headquarters office was established at the Chandler Mansion in Enfield, and surveys and test borings begun to determine what work was necessary to flood the valley. Dana, Enfield, Greenwich, and Prescott were to be eliminated for this project, and parts of seven other towns affected. Land purchases began in December, 1926.

The Ware River diversion project in the Barre area was constructed in the late 1920s, but the aqueduct west to the Swift River valley was not completed until 1933. Construction of the dam and dike at the southern ends of the Swift River valley did not get underway until the mid-1930s, after a diversion tunnel was built for the Swift River. A modern brick administration building was erected just west of the site of the dam in Belchertown.

Since millions of cubic yards of fill had to be used to build up the dam and dike, these took about two years each to complete. Meanwhile, buildings were being removed, and trees cut to prepare the future flow area for its fate. What trees could not be sold for timber and any brush left was piled up and burned. Access to the valley was restricted by the installation of gates across roads leading into it.

Everyone who was living within the flow area was moved out by the time flooding began on August 14, 1939. The last building removed within the flow area was the old Commission headquarters office in Enfield, in 1940. The access restrictions were kept in place during World War II for security reasons.

During that war, bomber aircraft from the Westover base in Chicopee used the reservoir basin for target practice. Artillery was tested in the southern part of the reservoir, and near the site of North Dana. The fence that was built across the northern end of the Prescott peninsula was intended to keep people away from the bombing targets. When the war ended, it was decided to leave the fence up so that the public could be kept out to create a wildlife sanctuary.

Quabbin Reservoir first overflowed the spillway east of the dam on June 22, 1946, reaching its 412 billion gallon capacity. The Water Commission was absorbed by the M.D.C. Water (later Watershed) Division in 1947. Shore fishing was permitted in 1946; boat fishing in 1952. Other than this, the general public has been allowed only hiking, and some bicycling at the Quabbin Reservation as recreational activities.

Management activities, including logging operations, have been carried on in the reservation since the 1930s. The handling of visitors was rather informal until the early 1980s. People with questions about historical matters were often referred to the Swift River Valley Historical Society in No, New Salem (begun in 1935).

The founding of the Friends of Quabbin, Inc.,

and the opening of the Quabbin Visitor's Center at the administration building occurred in 1984. There is now an Interpretive Services staff at the Visitor's Center. Informative displays and programs are held there.

Interest in the Quabbin boomed in the early 1980s, with the appearance of a documentary film and several books about it, and the reintroduction of the American Bald Eagle to the place. This last was accomplished by a special state program, corporate donations, and assistance from volunteers.

Since the early 1960s, there have been many proposals or efforts to open up the Quabbin for more public recreation. Activities ranging from sailboating, cross-country skiing, an excursion boat, large concerts, to swimming and camping have been sought by different groups. Public hearings on the five year recreation plans for Quabbin bring out many factions on these issues. There has been a legally constituted Quabbin Watershed Advisory Council since the early 1980s, which assists the M.D.C. in formulating its policies for the Quabbin.

Special deer hunts were conducted in the Quabbin Reservation in the early 1990s, but these were done to thin the herd to enhance watershed forest regeneration. The controversy over this activity raised questions about the whole management philosophy for the Quabbin Reservation.

In spite of the fact that many seem to want to "love Quabbin to death" in their own way, it is considered a special place by almost all who are familiar with it. This book is intended to make the human history of the place come alive for those who want to explore it.

Chapter 3 - QUABBIN PARK

Quabbin Park is the name given to the southernmost section of the Quabbin Reservation, located north of Route 9 in Belchertown and Ware. It is bounded on the north by the reservoir shoreline from the dam to the dike; on the west by the service road leading from Route 9 to the administration building at Winsor Dam; and on the east by the eastern boundary of the reservation lands running south from Gate 50 and Goodnough Dike to Route 9.

This 3,100 acre area includes nine miles of paved roads, and about eighteen miles of dirt roads and nature trails. There is a self-guiding forest stewardship trail behind the administration building. A booklet describing the stops on its 1 1/4 mile route is available. Other trails are found on a separate map of the park.

The administration building, visitor's center, state police station, and maintenance buildings are located just west of Winsor Dam. The lookout tower on top of Quabbin Mtn., and the maintenance building at the Quabbin Park Cemetery are the other major buildings here. There are many picnic spots and scenic vistas along the park's roads.

Quabbin Park is the most heavily "managed" part of the reservation, being the only one with public vehicle access, and adjacent to the major administration facilities. A study in the late 1980s placed the mumber of "person visits" to the park at around 600,000 per year. The spring and fall seem to be the most popular times of the year for people to come here.

Due to the siting of the dams, and the lack of villages within its bounds, Quabbin Park does not offer much to the history buff, unless one is interested in the engineering structures. However, there are a few places of historic interest worth noting here.

The Quabbin Visitor's Center was opened in 1984. It is located in the administration building just west of Winsor Dam. The Interpretive Services staff, or volunteers man the center yearound, including weekends. Based in one large room on the ground floor, the center contains visual displays, maps, and a small but growing collection of books, clippings, articles, oral history tapes, and other memorabilia on the human and natral history of the Quabbin. Arrangements can be made for staff to conduct programs at the center for groups. The Friends of Quabbin, Inc. is the support group for the center; it offers books, maps, and other items for sale there.

Quabbin Administration Bldg.(1940s)

The official records of the former valley towns, their real estate, and most of the files generated when the reservoir was constructed are stored in the administration building. Access to any of these is by special arrangement.

If you travel over Winsor Dam, from the Visitor's Center, take a left after the keystone arch bridge. This road passes by the spillway, and around a bay before heading up a steep hill. Part way up on the left is a small park, with a plaque set into a stone. This honors Frank E. Winsor, who was the chief engineer for the project from its beginning until his sudden death in 1939. Just above the park, there are plaques set into a ledge on the administration road. These commemorate the building of this road with Water Commission and federal (P.W.A,) funds in 1940.

Further up the hill is a rotary. The first right right leads up to the summit tower parking lot. The glassed-in observation floor of this 65 foot tall stone structure provides a nearly complete view of the reservoir on a clear day. A handsome villa owned by the Woods family was torn down to clear the way for this tower.

The second turn off the rotary leads onto the other side of the main access road. It goes down to the Enfield Lookout. There is a sign here with photographs showing what Enfield looked like when it was whole, and when it was torn down, but not yet flooded. About all that can be seen of the old village are a few of the upper terraces of the cemetery that was behind the Congregational Church. The saw blade that was used to make a sign here actually came from North Dana.

Enfield, Mass., around 1905

This lookout is considered one of the best spots at Quabbin for trying to spot the bald eagles during the winter months.

Another site of historical interest is located inside of the un-numbered Gate 52, which is on the main access road through the park, northwest of Goodnough Dike, and east of the Hanks picnic area. Park next to the gate (a wooden barway), and walk down the old paved road. This road was once state highway 109, connecting Ware and Belchertown through Enfield (the other end of the road emerges from the reservoir east of Gate 5).

There are brooks on either side as you walk down the road. Not far down the hill, you will notice some empty concrete structures and girders on the right. These were used during World War II to store ammunition for guns mounted on top of a platform. The shells were fired into the flooding valley, and their effectiveness (and the gunner's accuracy) were checked. Many guns made at the Springfield Armory were tested here.

After the war's end, the contents of the structures (and the platform) were removed. Since they were made of concrete, it was not deemed necessary or expedient to remove them. Today, you can walk on and around these abandoned bunkerlike ruins. A short distance below this point, the road goes into the water on its submerged route to the site of Enfield.

The other two sites of historical interest within Quabbin Park, the Webster Road and Quabbin Park Cemetery will be decribed in the following two chapters.

MAP OF QUABBIN PARK & WEBSTER ROAD

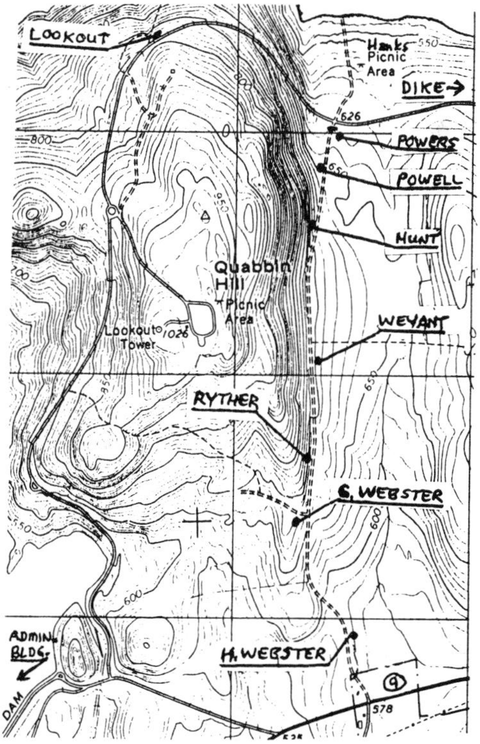

Chapter 4 - THE WEBSTER ROAD

In their zeal to try to limit and control access to the Quabbin Reservation, some M.D.C. administrators have encouraged the public to use Quabbin Park, and discourage them from visiting other watershed lands. This is partly due to the proximity to the headquarters buildings, and the ease in patrolling the area. With this idea in mind, the Webster Road has been promoted (since the late 1980s) as an "historic area," to steer hikers away from the more historic northern sections of the reservation. While this road has some cellarholes of interest, it lacks any village or mill sites.

To hike up the Webster Road (Walter Clark called it Long Hill Rd.), park at the lot at the Hanks picnic area (This is not always open during the winter months; then you have to pull over on the side of the paved road naer the gate). The Hanks farmstead was obliterated by the parking lot. Walk back up to the paved administration road. Across from you is a gated-off dirt road heading uphill into the woods; this is the Webster Road.

On the left side of the road, just inside the gate, is a row of six old pillar foundations. This was the Powers mansion, owned by David Blodgett in the mid-1800s. The latter's only son drowned as a young man while hauling ice from a pond in 1855. Azubah Palmer owned the 21-room house for a while in the 1870s-80s, then his estate sold it to L. J. Powers, a Springfield industrialist, in 1890.

Powers added six massive pillars to the front of the house. Donald Howe called it "Quaint Quabbin" in his book, and illustrates it on page 83. The style of this home is reminiscent of a southern plantation house.

Besides the pillar bases here, one can still see the cellarhole, front steps, the steps into the cellar. and the well. Parts of the foundations of attached sheds and a barn can also be located.

Proceeding further up the maple-lined road, there is a birch grove on the left, then an old

L.J. Powers' home *(MDC Photo)*

trash pile in a cellarhole. A logging road goes off to the left here. A. Bartlett owned this place in 1870. His son John committeed suicide by hanging himself in his barn in 1898. This home was gone before the reservoir came.

The next cellarholes are not far beyond, after breaks in the walls on both sides of the road. This was Clinton Powell's 49 acre farm. The 1 1/2 story cape-style house was on the right. It had an ell, and was partly brick. The home was built in the late 1700s; earlier owners included Reuben Lazell, Barnabas Blair (from 1829-57; he was a selectman for a time), Nathan Weeks, Daniel Fisk, and A. Bartlett (1870s-90s). Powell's wife Leila was apparently a niece of Lydia Bartlett. There was a barn and two sheds across the road; the cement foundation of a milk tank is still visible.

Clinton Powell, 1910

Powell, a dairy farmer and auctioneer, was a native of New York state. His pride in how he kept up his farm was evident in his remark to a news reporter; "You never once have to raise the cutter bar when cutting hay in my fields." A relative who often visited him was 1930s movie actress and dancer Eleanor Powell. He moved an Enfield house to Monson after settling with the Water Commission in December, 1938.

Proceeding up the road, the next cellarholes were the farm of Henry and Harriet Hunt after 1907. The 2 1/2 story house was on the right; the filled-in cellarhole is above a stone wall. There was a barn across the road. This was Augustus T. Tuttle's from the 1850s to 1900. Tuttle ran a business in Holyoke, selling butter, fruit, and poultry produced here.

An old lane runs to the east from here, with a stone wall along the north side. The Rohan farm (H. Pittsinger's in the 1850s) was at the end of this lane in the late 1800s. A trail continues from there toward Goodnough Dike.

The next cellarhole was on a small farm bordered by stone walls on all but one side. A cement step on the right is the easiest remnant to find. An indistinct barn cellarhole on the knoll to the right was part of a farm owned by Henry Fobes in the 1850s. Daniel Juckett sold it to H. C. M. Howe in 1883.

The house was on the left; the cellarhole was

H.C.M. Howe Home, c1905

obliterated. This property passed to H.C.M. Howe's daughter, Lillian Weyant in 1899. She was a professor of elocution at Wesleyan Academy. The Webber family was renting here when it burned in the 1920s. The property was sold to the Water Commission by Weyant's brother, Edwin H. Howe.

There is a stonewall - lined lane off to the left at the southern end of the Howe lots. Just past this, on the right, are three cellarholes on a rise. These were outbuildings of the Martindale farm, which is profiled after the next site.

A few hundred feet past the outbuilding cellarholes, on the left, is a lane. There is one cellarhole just inside the lane, on the right, and two jast past it on the left. This was H.C.M. Howe's first farm, from the 1850s until he moved to the place we have just passed. The buildings were cellarholes when Henry Hunt sold this property to the Water Commission.

Just past this site is another lane off to the left. A stone wall lines the north side of it. This leads to a trail that goes over a mile to the access road south of Goodnough Dike.

The next site is just past this lane, on the right. It has the most intriguing story of the places on this road. Here are several filled-in cellarholes of the house, and several barns and outbuildings. Part of a field is still open. This was the farm of the Fobes and the Martindales.

Jesse Fobes came here from Bridgewater in 1796. He brought his family (including young Henry), a yoke of oxen, and a horse and wagon. He concealed the money to pay for the farm with some oats in a kettle. When Enfield became a town in 1816, Jesse Fobes was one of the first Selectmen. Jesse's son Charles (who added an "r" to his last name), became a distinguished Northampton jurist. He bequeathed the ornate library building that bears his name to his adopted city.

Henry Fobes was a veteran of the War of 1812, for wehich he reecived a pension of $8.00 a month in his last years. He also served the town as a Selectmen for several terms, was a deacon of the Congregational Church, and a master of the Bethel Masonic Lodge.

Joel W. and William F. Martindale purchased this

farm from the elderly Henry Fobes in 1870, for $8,000. They gave Fobes $2,500 in cash, and notes for the rest. Fobes "relinquished $3,000 (of the purchase price) for depreciation," so they gave him a note for $2,000 for the balance. Fobes was to destroy the note if the Martindales fed and housed him there for the rest of his life.

Martindale Farm or "Maple Terrace"
(from Evert's History, 1879)

H.M. Woods, Henry Fobes' guardian, sued the Martindales for $2,000 in 1883, claiming that they had "unfairly" influenced Fobes to give up the note. The trial was held in Superior Court at Northampton, under Judge Staples. During the the two-week long trial, Fobes testified that he was "satisfied" with the arrangement over the note. The Martindales were found not guilty.

When Fobes died in 1885, he was just under 93 years old. He left considerable sums of money to the church and the town.

Joel Martindale married Mary J. Webster; they had a son and six daughters. They named the farm "Maple Terrace." In the late 1870s. it was considered one of the finer farms in Enfield.

In 1917, Emory Bartlett, a grandson of Joel, took over the place, and incorporated it as Martindale Farms, Inc. In 1925, ownership of the farm passed into the hands of Enfield businessman H. Morgan Ryther (reportedly in settlement of debts for grain purchased).

When the Water Commission was planning land purchases for the reservoir, it was determined that this farm should be taken, even though it was outside of the watershed. However, since Martha Martindale Vining (born 1874) and her sister Mary Martindale (born 1875) were both still living there, an agreement was made to let them remain on the farm as long as they lived.

Their nephew, Emory Bartlett, now a Commission employee, looked after them. Folllwing the death of both women in the 1950s, the buildings were torn down.

During World War II, the Water Commission attempted to save fuel and manpower by purchasing a flock of sheep. It was hoped that their grazing on the grassy slopes of the dam structures and adjoining fields would keep the grass down. During the cold months of the year, the sheep were kept in the several barns and sheds on the Martindale farm. The sheep were sold off after the war, as they were not efficient enough to keep.

Not far past the Martindale place is a large cement cellarhole near the road on the right. This was one of the farm barns; there were two sheds behind it.

A few hundred feet past the barn cellarhole is a lane off to the right, This is the beginning of a hiking trail that connects up with trails toward Quabbin Hill, or to the spillway east of Winsor Dam.

Just off the Webster Road on this lane is the site of the George Webster farm. This was a 1 1/2 story house, with an ell and attached barn, plus outbuildings. A cement watering trough is still visible here, as is the filled-in barn cellarhole.

George's father Jedidiah settled here in 1843. According to Donald Howe, George Webster was an innovative agriculturalist and animal breeder,who ran his farm with electricity he generated there. His wife was the former Louise Martindale. George Webster was the oldest man in town when he died at 86 in 1932.

George Webster's granddaughter Trudy Ward Stalbird Terry married a junior engineer on the Quab-

George Webster Home *(MDC Photo)*

bin project. She was often seen at Quabbin valley reunions and at the "Tuesday Teas" held at the Visitor's Center in the 1980s and 1990s.

The Webster Road goes down a hill and around a curve after George Webster's place. Where the stone wall ends on the left is the former boundary line bewteen Enfield and Ware. There is a reclaimed field on the left here, with three cellarholes in it. This was the farm of George Webster's son Henry. The house was a small 1 1/2 story place.

A wetland is visible through the trees behind Henry Webster's cellarholes. Route 9 passes over a causeway across this wetland. The unnumbered Gate 53 is just south of Webster's. The home just outside of the gate is on private property.

Chapter 5 – QUABBIN PARK CEMETERY

This cemetery is located off Route 9, just west of the entrance to the Goodnough Dike approach road. The large vault is near the entrance. A curved dirt road leads up to the cemetery. Over 6,500 of the bodies removed from cemeteries in the Swift River valley were reinterred here.

Burials still take place here, as anyone who had a plot in a valley cemetery could have it transferred to here. Engineers and former employees at Quabbin are also buried at this cemetery, which has a capacity for over 11,000 graves.

At the top of the hill on the access road, there is a group of monuments that came from towns in the valley. These are cannons from Dana and Enfield, Enfield's Civil War statue, and the war memorial and Ballou plaques from Dana Common.

Statue, Cannon, and Cannonballs in Enfield
(Dana Monuments & Cannon pictured in Chapter 16)

The cemetery is very nicely landscaped, with dirt roads providing access to the grave plots. Unfortunately, the graves were not put in any particular order - not even by town! A building on the northwest edge of the cemetery houses the burial records and equipment.

A walk among these gravestones may seem eerie, especially when it is realized that the living were not the only ones disturbed by the reservoir project!

Chapter 6 - PACKARDVILLE (GATE 8)

Packardville was a hamlet on the Pelham side of the boundary with Enfield. When it began to form in the 1830s, several of the residents were Packards, giving the place its name. To reach this site, park at Gate 8, which is on the Packardville Rd., east of Route 202 in southern Pelham. The gate is open during daylight hours between mid-April and mid-October, as the road leads to the boat launch site at Fishing Area #1. However, no parking is allowed until the boat launch area.

Walking in from Gate 8, the first cellarhole is about a quarter mile in on the left. This was the first of two houses on this road owned by William Chaffee (P. Bartlett's in the 1850s; J.W. Keith's in 1870). The large, two section house had a porch on the right facing the road. There was a shed behind the house, and a large barn and sheds across the road.

Another fifth of a mile down the road on the left is the cellarhole of the Dorcas Collis heirs (W. Randall's in 1855, J. W. Keith's in 1870). This was a 1 1/2 story cape, with an ell; a barn was on the right side of the road. Alice Collis, a daughter of Dorcas, was one of the last teachers at the South School in Pelham (at Gate 9).

Collis House and Family *(Pelham Historical Soc.)*

A site on the left not far after the Collis place was a district school in the 1850s. Another site a short distance down the road on the left was the Butler place in the 1850s, then Deacon Albert Firman's in the late 1800s; it was gone before the reservoir came.

There were only three homes at the crossroads by the time the reservoir came. The William Chaffee place (H. Ward's in the 1850s, P. Bartlett's in 1870) was on the north side of the road west of the crossroads; the barns were on the opposite side of the road.

The road to the left at the crossroads is the Davis Road. It goes about three miles northward to a junction with the road from Gate 11. The third cellarhole on the left about a mile north of the village (Ellison Dodge's in the mid-1800s) was the site of the famous Montgomery child murder in 1882. (For details, see Chapter 42 in the author's 1993 book *"Strange Tales From Old Quabbin."*). Two lefts off Davis Road lead to Gates 9 and 10, (see next chapter). There is one road to the right (Governors Woods Road West) before The Davis Road joins the road from Gate 11.

Juckett Hill Road runs to the right at the Packardville crossroads. It heads in a southerly direction, towards Gate 7 (a road to the right) and Gate 6 (two miles away in northeast Belchertown).

Back at the crossroads, the cellarhole of the A. Hanks place in 1870 is on the northeast corner of the crossroads. The open cellarhole of the Ward place is on the southeast corner; a brook runs behind it. This small 1 1/2 story building was J. Hanks' store from 1860 to 1873. The wagon shop operated by Packard and Thurston in the early 1840s was located here.

A gated-off road to the right after the crossroads has a couple of cellarholes on it. The homes were gone before the reservoir came.

Henry Stevens' home (Randall's in 1854, J. Hanks' in 1870) was about 300 feet east of the crossroads, on the south side of the road. A hundred feet east of Stevens home, and 150 feet south of the road is the cellarhole of the Packardville Union Church. A horse barn was behind this edifice, which was just inside the boundary line in Enfield. There was also a small cemetery here, which had 22 graves.

A Baptist parish was formed here and a church built in 1831. A hamlet grew up around it, based upon the short-lived wagon factory and a shingle mill. By 1860, there wern't enough Baptists to keep up the church, so it combined with Congregationalists and Methodists to form a Union parish.

Packardville Church

In January, 1869, this was reorganized as a Union Congregational Church, and repairs were begun. Unfortunately. the church burned in a suspicious fire that April, which also destroyed the shingle mill. The church was soon rebuilt, and dedicated on June 28, 1871. Rev. William Vaille was installed as the minister; he also served the Pelham Center church. His daughter taught in Enfield schools. Unfortunately, the parish was so small, it soon had to rely upon divinity students from nearby Amherst College to do the preaching.

In May, 1921, lightning struck the church just as the Sunday School class was beginning. No one was injured, but the church received minor damage. S. Alice Collis was the last of three long-serving clerks (the other two were Mr. and Mrs. Darius Chickering) for this parish.

The last service was held here on June 7, 1936, after the Mass. Congregational Conference and Missionary Society sold the church to the Water Commission. The church bell was moved to Amherst College, then to Dwight Chapel in Belchertown.

The road to the left just past here joins the road north out of the crossroads in a short distance. Along the right side of this road is the cellarhole of the old Thayer home, formerly owned by D. Packard. This was gone before the reservoir came, the land being sold to the state by Stanton Fleming. Just across from this, in the woods on the left, was the village cemetery, which held 209 graves. Many of the boundary posts are still standing.

A few hundred feet north of the cemetery site are three cellarholes; two on the left (barns), and one on the right at a break in the stonewall (the homestead). These were owned by the Packard family for several decades, being sold out at the end by Elbridge Packard. The latter's ancestor, Walter Packard ("The Man Who Hung Himself Twice") is the subject of Chapter 38 in the author's 1993 book *"Strange Tales From Old Quabbin."*

Back along the main road toward the boat lauch ramp, a stream runs alongside to the right. This is Cadwell Creek, the only named "creek" in Hampshire County.

There is a cellarhole on the left not far before a road junction. This was the Jeremiah & Mary Day place, known as Sunnybrook Farm. It was the home of M. Torrance in the 1850s, and D.F. Packard in 1870. Torrance also made shingles at his mill, which burned in 1853. The house was 1 1/2 stories, in two sections, with a porch on the front and right side. There was a barn to the right of it.

The road on the left is called Governors Woods Rd.; it goes north for over three miles to meet the road from Gate 11. A road to the left about a mile north of here joins up with the Davis Road on its way toward the Gate 11 road.

Continuing on the road toward the fishing area, there is a cellarhole site past the junction on the left. The house (W. Hanks in 1870) was gone before the reservoir came.

The next group of cellarholes (at breaks in the stone walls) was the Chickering family farm from 1813. Otis Chickering ran a sawmill on the creek in the middle 1800s; the mill dam can still be seen. Bertrand Chickering, who sold the property to the Water Commission, ran the telephone exchange in Enfield for amny years. The barns were on the right, before the house, which was on the left. This was a fine 2 1/2 story home, with bay windows, and a 1 1/2 story ell. It was built in 1881, to replace a home that burned.

Chickering Home

The next cellarhole was on the left after the road crosses Chaffee Brook, on a hill about 300 feet off the road. This was the George Dunbar place, owned by E.Richards in the 1850s, and Mrs. Randall in 1870. The 2 1/2 story house had a barn near it.

After going further down the hill, you will come to the shore at Fishing Area #1. There is a fee to park a vehicle here, whether one fishes or not. From this parking lot, one can see the summit tower on Quabbin Hill, Winsor Dam, and the administration building.

There is an obliterated cellarhole located on the left edge of the parking lot near the shoreline, along the original roadway. This was the Alice Parsons place, owned by D. H. Bartlett in the 1850s, and one Needham in 1870. This was a 1 1/2 story cape, with a two story extension, and a barn. Alice Parsons was the first property owner in the valley to offer to sell out to the Water Commission in 1926.

MAP OF PACKARDVILLE AREA

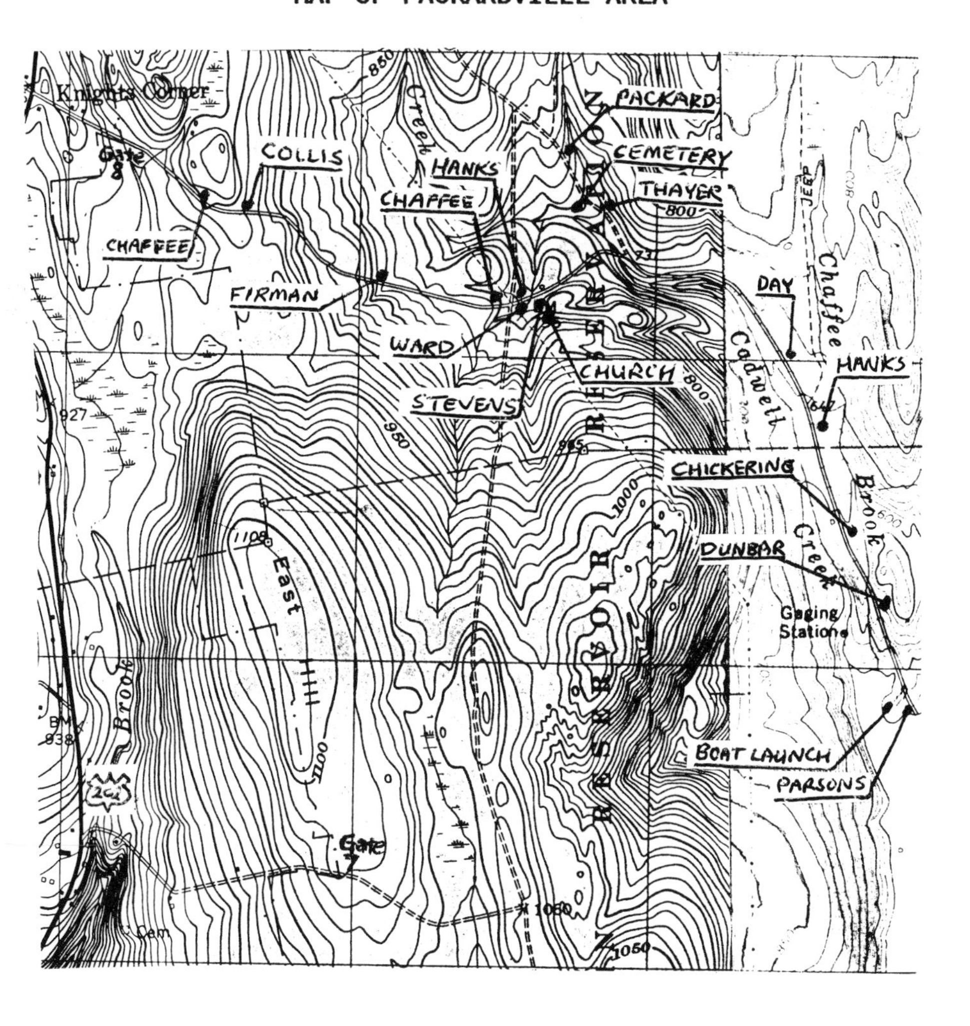

Chapter 7 - EAST PELHAM - GATE 11

This gate is located on the east side of Route 202, across from Pelham Center. Most of the buildings that made up the eastern side of this village were taken for watershed protection. This is also the closest gate to the heavily populated Amherst area, so it is hiked by many people.

To hike down this road, park where it begins, off the Daniel Shays Highway (U. S. Route 202). Across the street from here is the Congregational Church. the old burial ground, and the 1743 Town Hall, which is claimed to be the oldest one in continuous use in New England.

The road passing through Gate 11 was part of the old Sixth Massachusetts Turnpike, which was chartered in 1799. The corporation had to improve existing roads, or build new sections to connect them in following a prescribed route. This road was completed in 1800, running from Amherst on the west, following the current Amherst-Pelham road to this gate, then down the hill, across the West Branch of the Swift River into what became Prescott in 1822. The road ran eastward through Greenwich and Hardwick toward its ultimate destination in Shrewsbury.

Tolls were levied for through travelers and freight haulers, the rates depending upon the size of the vehicle or number of animals pulling it. These varied from one to 25 cents. Toll gates were located about every ten miles. One was in Pelham Center, and another just east of Greenwich Village. The section of the road in Pelham and Greenwich was removed from the turnpike company's control in 1820,becoming a county road.

Since the Water Commission purchased almost all of the property in the town east of Route 202, four homes at the beginning of this road are now cellarholes. In 1933, Pelham Selectman Edward Boyden asked the Water Commission if these homes could be spared so that this part of town "could continue to be a community center." Chief Engineer Frank E. Winsor agreed, citing the fact that they were 7,500 feet away from the shoreline, and were "no measurable sanitary menace." However, the possibility that some of these properties might be subdivided into several houselots (taking advantage of the view) caused the Commission to purchase them later.

The first home on the north side of the junction was the Martin Kingman Tavern from at least the early 1820s to 1838. Kingman also ran a store here in the 1830s; he was postmaster from 1824-40. Calvin Eaton succeeded Kingman, but ran the tavern for only a few years. He continued the store business for many years, and served as postmaster from 1840-60. Ariel C. Keith, town clerk for many years, bought this in 1870. Robert and Eva Richardson were the last owners.

Kingman Tavern

This 14 room 2 1/2 story building was reportedly offered to the Town of Pelham for municipal use, perhaps as an historical museum, but this was turned down. The town did vote to ask the Commission to spare the building, and received assurances that it would not be torn down. In 1944, much to the town's surprise, Stephen Racz, of the Milford (CT) Antique Shop was allowed to buy the the tavern building, barn, and garage and remove them for $375.00. Part of the tavern building (including the spring dance floor) is now a chicken coop on a farm near Pelham Center. The tavern site is now a small field; the house and barn cellarholes are barely discernable.

The house on the southeast side of this road junction was last owned by Almira Keep, then Eleanor Struthers. Earlier owners included J. Parents (1850s), and D.F. Packard (1870). It was a 1 1/2 story home, with an ell. There was barn behind it, and one to the south; all of the cellarholes are filled in; it is now a field.

Proceeding down the road before the turn, there are cellarholes on both sides of the road. The filled-in one way in the field on the right was the two story Georgianna Cook residence; there was a shed next to the road. This was Job S. Miller's home in the 1850s, H. Abercrombie's in 1870. Several fine shade trees still stand here.

The first set of two cellarholes on the left was a place owned by B. Benjamin in 1870, later by the Keiths. It, and the barn behind it were gone before the reservoir came.

The the next cellarhole on the left was partly damaged when the parking area across from the gate was dug out. This was sold by Peter Benjamin to Myrett Boynton in 1874. A second cellarhole on this property is just to the left of the gate. This building dated from about 1845. A store was run by C. Wheeler on the first floor, and a boot shop on the second. Later store proprietors were William Conkey, Job Miller, and E. S. Richardson (postmaster from 1860-67). Myrett Boynton ran this from 1866, and served as postmaster from 1867-69, and 1870-1904. This building burned in 1895.

Boynton's Store *(MDC Photo)*

Boynton rebuilt his store on the first cellarhole, as a 1 1/2 story structure with a porch. The post office closed in 1910. George F. Storrs, then Edward Hunter were the last owners of this property. There was a barn in back, and a shed to the east.

After passing through the gate, the road goes down a hill. There is a logging road on the left, then an old road on the right, which led to an old cellarhole. This was the Silas Shores place in 1870.

The next cellarhole on the turnpike road is on the left, about a half mile in from the gate,just before a road junction. This was the J. Smith place in the 1850s, and Harrison Horr's in 1870. The last owner was the John Ely Estate. It was a 1 1/2 story cape, with two sheds in the back.

The road to the right just past the Ely place is the Davis Road. It passes by several cellarholes over its three mile route southward toward Packardville. About a third of a mile down this road are the cellarholes of a farm owned by the Davis family for several decades. The classic 2 1/2 story "I" house was on the right; there were barns on the left.

Samuel Davis Home
(*Parmenter's History of Pelham*)

In another third of a mile, the Davis Road comes to a junction with the Governors Woods Road (West). This left heads toward the road to Fishing Area #1. The cellarholes at this fork were part of the summer home of Thomas Costello, a Springfield man. The 1 1/2 story gabled house was on the left; the barn was on the right. This was A. Taylor's place in the middle 1800s.

In another third of a mile, a road to the right off the Davis Road leads to Gate 10. There are many high-bush blueberry bushes in this area. Only one set of cellarholes is located on this road, which was the old Moses L. Ward farm. The obliterated cellarhole of the 2 1/2 story house was on the right (north side), at a corner in the road. The barn was on the left side of the road. Lysander Ward (M.L.'s son) was the mailman for Pelham for many years in the early 1900s. He had moved to a home near the center before this place burned around 1927.

Gate 10 is on Route 202, about 1 1/3 miles south of Pelham Center, so a loop hike is possible a-long the grassy area alongside of the highway.

Resuming our journey down the old turnpike road, from the junction with the Davis Road, there is another site just past the junction on the left. This was H. Abercrombie's in 1854, and T.W. Stratton's in 1870. It was gone before the reservoir came.

About 600 feet past the junction, there is an old road off to the right. This went for about a half mile to the Mary Miller house and barn (J. Whitney's in 1870).

Just after this road junction is the site of East School, on the left. This one-room school was used from 1867-1934. The building was moved to Amherst after the Commission purchased the property; only a remnant of the chimney remains.

East Pelham School

Not far after the school, on the left, is the site of the S. Bailey farm in the 1850s. It was gone by 1870. A stone-lined "beehive structure" is just east of the cellarhole. The sharp corner here was called "Deck Bend."

Around the corner there is an old road to the left; this led to what was the A. Hutchinson place in 1870. The cellarhole on the Turnpike road to the right here was the J. Cutting place in the mid-1800s. The home was gone before the reservoir came.

Not far past the Cutting place, on the left, was the Albert Frost farm (Lorin Woods' from 1869-90). The 1 1/2 story house and several barns and sheds were on the left; a couple of sheds were on the right. Over the years, the Frosts operated at least two mills in Pelham Hollow in the early 1900s, making pegs, whip handles, and shingles.

Frost Farm on left

(Clifton Johnson photo, Jones Library)

The Frosts disputed the appraisal of Water Commission; They wanted $90,000 for their 115 acres scattered around Pelham and Prescott. A court case was necessary to settle the dispute for a smaller sum. Some of the family moved to Pelham Center after leaving this place.

Just after the Frost's, a road goes off to the right. Sometimes called the Montgomery Road, the M.D.C. dubbed it the Governors Woods Road (East).

This runs southward for over two miles to join the road from Gate 8 not far above the boat launch area. There are several cellarholes along its length.

There is an M.D.C.- made road on the left after this. It connects with the road that ran along the north bank of Purgee Brook, which can be reached from Gate 12. A very old millsite is near where the road crosses the brook.

The last cellarholes on the turnpike road before it goes into the reservoir are about a third of a mile past the road junction, on the left at a slight curve. This was the Joseph and Delima Marion farm. Earlier owners included L. Chapin (1850s), S. Chamberlain (1870), and Grace Hatt (1916). The 1 1/2 story house was to the left and behind the large tree, which is still standing. It had an ell on the right. A barn was located over 100 feet behind the house, close to Purgee Brook Bay in the reservoir.

Marion Home *(MDC Photo)*

Joseph Marion filed his property form with the Water Commission in February, 1927. Three months later, Marion inquired why no action had been taken on it, which revealed that the form had been misplaced. On the form, he noted that he had built an icehouse, a gas lighting plant, and had done many repairs and improvements to the property, which cost him almost as much as he had paid for the place 11 years earlier. He also added the following plaintive statement:

"I am by trade a blacksmith, with a shop at my home and also in Greenwich, Mass., the only blacksmith shop within a radius of seven miles. The reservoir not only takes my home away and one by one as claims are settled all my customers. My business has given me an average of $1000 a year, but in arriving at the selling price of my property, $8,000, I have taken into consideration the present and future damage done my business. Because of the incresasing damage done my business, I desire a settlement at the earliest possible date."

Like almost everyone else in the valley, Marion was not compensated for his loss of business. However, he may have had the satisfaction of knowing that the Water Commission had to spend a great deal of time disuntangling his defective property title, and in getting his children to sign off on their shares of his deceased wife's half of the property.

Under the waters of the reservoir, about 200 feet from the shoreline, was the site of the Pelham Hollow crossroads. The old school, and several homes were located here. The bridge over the West Branch of the Swift River was another fifth of a mile to the east. The history of the mills in this village (and the rest of Pelham) are recalled in Paul Bigelow's excellent 1993 book *"Wrights and Privileges."*

MAP OF EAST PELHAM

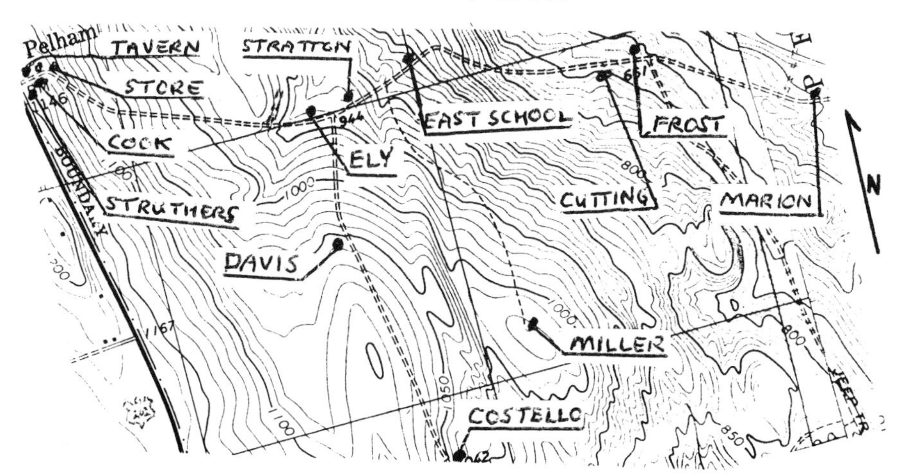

Chapter 8 - PUPPYVILLE (GATE 22)

The former New Salem village of Puppyville was located just inside of Gate 22, in the southern part of New Salem. The first grist mill in New Salem was reportedly built here in the mid-1700s.

This gate can be reached via Freeman Road off U.S. Route 202; a sign here directs one to "So. New Salem." This road is about a mile south of the Hamilton Orchards sign. There is a sign for a maple sugar business at the beginning of this road. Proceed down it, bear right at a junction, then left at two more junctions. The road to the right at the third junction leads to Gate 20, at the site of North Prescott village. All that remains there are a couple of homes, and the old village cemetery.

The final left road passes by a couple of homes, then comes to Gate 22. Park near here, then walk inside the gate. The road to the right led up the hill in the direction of North Prescott. It was open to public travel before being gated off in the 1980s. The village school once stood part way up the hill on the left.

Continuing down the hill, there are home sites on either side of the road between crossing two brooks. The first one on the right was a small cottage called the "Yellow House." Elon Haskins owned this in the 1850s. The 1871 map calls this C.F.Carpenter's, although Mager Brown owned it in

MacGregor Home

the late 1800s. Rob Roy McGregor was the last owner, buying this from Edward Turner in 1926.

The first cellarhole (filled-in) on the left was Elon Haskins' 6 room home and blacksmith shop in the mid-1800s. Dr. Albert Haskins and his sister Carrie last lived here. The second cellarhole on the left was Elon Haskins' saw mill, which utilized the waterpower of Hop Brook. A part of the millrace is still discernable next to the bridge.

Just before the brook on the right was the Leander Keddie place after 1926. It was a 1 1/2 story home with 18 rooms. It had an ell on the right, and a barn to the right of that. It was owned by Elbridge Shaw in the 1850s, J.H. Carpenter in the 1870s, and Albert Hanson in the 1880s.

The village here originally went under the name "Coolidgeville," after Haskins' predecessor, who ran a shingle mill. According to local historian Florence Cox, the name Puppyville (used as early as 1863) was applied to it because "it is said a man once lived there who had a lot of puppies." A 1912 visitor to the area suggested that "Millington and Puppyville should exchange names, for while Puppyville has no dogs at all, Millington was overloaded with them."

Hop Brook, which is crossed here, once flowed into a pond of that name near the village of Millington. In his entertaining book, "Trout Waters," William Foye calls this stream Tyre Brook, a local nickname. The first stone bridge over Hop Brook here (known as the Hadley bridge) was erected in the early 1860s; it was washed away in an 1863 flood.

After crossing over Hop Brook, there are two homesites on the left side of the road as one proceeds up the small hill. The 7 room Furneaux place was at the foot of the hill, in a brush tangle. This was a story and a half cottage, with a long ell and attached shed; a barn was at the left. Earlier residents were E. Vaughan (1857), C.H. Brown (1870), and J.A. Titus (1871-99). Furneaux bought it in 1913. The South New Salem Social Club met here in 1916.

The 8 room Martha Johnson place was part way up the hill. This was a two and a half story house, with a porch along the east side, and an attached ell behind that. Previous residents included E. G. Hanson (1857), and Mager Brown (1865-99). The latter came to this area from Holden in the late 1830s, selling clocks.

Puppyville from the East (From left; Keddie's,Haskins', and Johnson's homes)

Near the top of the hill, there is an impressive stone wall off to the right side of the road, which was part of Whitney Haskins property (from 1901-22). The partly filled-in cellarhole of the 1830s 8 room house is at the top of the hill on the right; next to some spruces. This home was a 2 1/2 story structure, with aa ell and a large barn just to the left of it. Earlier owners included Napoleon B. Coolidge (who ran the village mill). Edward Felton, and H. and C. Coolidge. The last owner was Nellie Eaton. This home was left standing until the 1960s, as it was leased out to M.D.C. employees as a residence.

There is a road across from the Eaton place, which comes from a junction of roads from Gates 23 & 24. On the northwest side of this junction are stone walls in the banking that look like an old root cellar or storage place. A cellarhole behind this was the site of the old Cook Tavern, which flourished in the early 1800s.

On our main road, just past the Haskins place, on the same side of the road, is a very modern-looking concrete foundation. This was actually the original New Salem headquarters building for the M.D.C. in the 1950s and early 1960s. It was torn down after the current building was erected on Elm St. in North New Salem.

The homesite a few hundred feet down the street opposite the Haskins place was owned by Louis and Edith Nelson as a rental home. Sarah Shaw lived here in the 1850s, Miss Horr in the 1870s; later Damon Brown and Fred Goodale. This was a small 1 1/2 story cape, with a barn and shed in back. The well-site behind this supplied water for the former M.D.C. headquarters nearby.

Past a small downslope in the road on the right was the 2 1/2 story Comerford place. Daniel V. Putnam lived here in the mid-1800s; later Varney Putnam and Charles and Ella Wheeler. Charles Comerford (through his father) bought it from the New England Box Co., who owned the woodland behind it. When the Water Commission asked him to list his property for sale, he wrote,

> "I bought this property as nice land as any in the state intending to build and be near our relatives, but it was decided to flow this valley, and having my savings invested in same I am at a standstill until I sell in order to turn myself."

This 10 room residence had a couple of sheds in back. Joseph Russell, in his "Buildings and Bells" book, says that this large home was moved to Dorset, Vt., then moved again to Manchester, Vt. There is a charming path behind the cellar-

Commerford Home *(MDC Photo)*

hole through the woods that comes out on the road to Hop Brook mentioned in the next paragraph.

A fork in the road comes up soon after this. The road to the right runs downhill to the site of a old bridge over Hop Brook, just above where it flows into the reservoir. There is a charming pool just below the bridge site. Is this the spot admired by Evelina Gustafson in her *"Ghost Towns 'Neath Quabbin Reservoir"* book (on page 73)?

The New England Box Company once owned the land on both sides of this road as a timber lot. The road goes into the water after the bridge site.

Continuing down the road to the left from the junction, it goes down toward the shore of the reservoir. The old L.T. Briggs cellarhole is just past a brook on the right. Dexter Briggs sold this to E.W. Vineca in 1907. The Israel Ellis family was renting it when it burned in 1911.

Near the shoreline of the reservoir, there is a crossroads; the old Shaw cellarhole is located on the northeast side. The roads to the right and straight (towards the site of Millington) here go into the water. The road on the left, Paige Lane, heads northward along the attractive wooded shoreline for a mile to a junction. This road (covered in Chapter 9) makes a loop hike of several miles possible, via. Gate 26 and New Salem Center.

MAP OF PUPPYVILLE - GATE 22 AREA

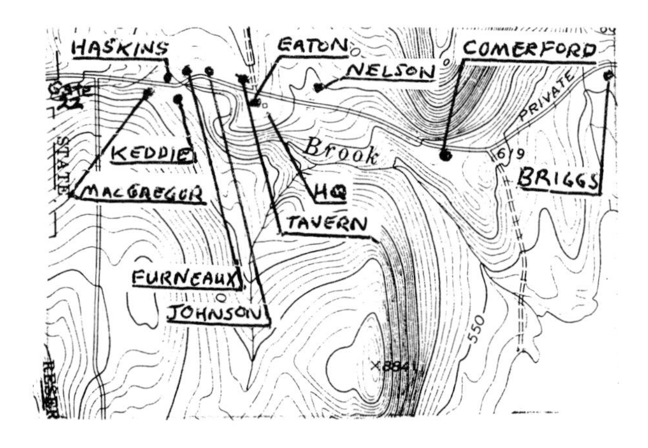

Chapter 9 - SOUTHEAST NEW SALEM (GATES 26-7)

This area, off East Main St. in New Salem, was not a village or a hamlet, but there are some interesting cellarholes here. It is between the areas described in the preceeding and next chapters, but is far enough away from them to merit separate coverage.

To reach Gate 26 and 27, take the road to New Salem Center off Route 202. You will come to a junction known as Reddy's Five Corners. In the late 1800s, a sign board was placed in the middle of this junction, with locations noted in four directions. Today, the signboard is at the Swift River Valley Historical Society Museum.

At the junction, go down East Main St. This is a steep hill, with a few peeks at the reservoir through openings in the trees. In less than a mile, Gate 27 (Beldin Hill Road) is on your left; Gate 26 is shortly after it. (The M.D.C. has proposed moving Gate 26 up next to Gate 27; as of early 1994, this move had not taken place.)

The dirt road past Gate 26 goes down hill over a mile before going into the water. There is a logging road ton the right just inside the gate. About 3/4 of a mile down the hill, a fine set of cement steps alert you to a cellarhole on the right, just before a road crossing. This was Elisha W. Vineca's home. Earlier owners included Calvin Hunt and Hartwell Crowl; Vineca's wife was

E. W. Vineca's home *(MDC Photo)*

a Crowl. The open cellarhole was of a 12 room house; there are also two large barn cellarholes. There was a garage, and henhouses on the property. Across the road from the cellarhole is a barway; a well is visible inside of it.

Vineca ran a store and was postmaster in North Dana from 1888-1891. After he sold out, he relocated here, becoming a large landowner in New Salem. Vineca carried on the Crowl Fern business. This enterprise was begun in the 1890s by Cyrus Crowl and the future Mrs. Vineca. It consisted of gathering laurel, ferns, and various greens, which were stored, or made into "roping." In holiday seasons, the greens were shipped out to florists over much of the northeast.

Vineca took over this business in 1912, and outlasted a rival concern operating out of Millington. The business continued to thrive into the early 1930s, even though the 12 room house and some sheds burned in 1928.

The left at this crossroads is the road back to the Beldin Hill Road mentioned earlier. The road going straight down the hill goes into the water in a few hundred feet. The road to the right, Paige Lane, follows the shoreline for a mile.

Just south of the crossroads on Paige Lane is a tall tree on the left. The wooden crossbeam and metal support arms are the mute testimony of a power or telephone line that was once here.

About a half mile down Paige Lane on the left is the site of Clayton Fisher's 5 room summer home after 1910. Pieces of the brick chimney are visible next to the open cellarhole. The barn cellarhole is partially visible across the way. Earlier occupants of this 1 1/2 story cape with an ell were the Solon and Wilson Lee families, J. Goodnow, H. Smith, and Nelson Bliss.

A few hundred feet south of the Fisher place was the 119 acre William Bliss farm. The 2 1/2 story, 8 room home, on the left, had a porch. The cement garage foundation is in front of the large open house cellarhole.

There were two barns beside the road, just south of the end of a stone wall; the foundations are gone. The shoreline is visible 200 feet behind the house cellarhole. Earlier inhabitants of this farm included L. Shaw, and G. W. Bliss.

In another quarter of a mile, this lane meets the road from Gate 22 at a crossroads (See Chapter 8).

Returning to Gate 27, there is a partially filled-in cellarhole to the right of the gate. This was the 7 room home of Frank Sampson, built in 1930 on land that had been in the family since 1908.

Beldin Hill Road goes down hill to a junction. The road straight ahead passes two sets of cellarholes on the left on its way down to the causeway over Moosehorn Brook bay. This joins up with the paved road from Gates 29-30 (See Chapter 10), making a loop hike of several miles in length possible.

The two cellarholes mentioned were owned by the Giles family in the 1870s. The first one was the home of Samuel Giles, who was a State senator in 1846. His daughter Abby married Moses Herrick, who ran the tavern not far away (see Chapter 10). Another daughter, Harriet, was one of the founders of the Spellman Seminary in Atlanta, GA.

Going back to the junction, there are several interesting cellarholes on the right side. The first of these is before the junction on the right. This was the 2 1/2 story home of Frank Sampson, which had an ell near the front. William Parkhurst built this house for his daughter Mary in the late 1800s.

The next homes were on the left immediately after taking the right at the junction. The first open cellarhole was the 4 room, 1 1/2 story home of Alice Sampson. Earlier owners were William Parkhurst (from c1850-1888), the Ramsdells, and Jennie Giffin Cummings, who sold it to the Sampsons in 1918. On her listing form, Alice Sampson asked the Commission to "please act on this as soon as possible, as we are old people and want to get something else."

The next open cellarhole, just east of Alice Sampson's was the 4 room, 1 1/2 story George Sampson, Jr. place after 1918. Like the Alice Sampson place, this one had been owned by W. W. Parkhurst in the late 1800s; Frank Sampson owned it from 1908-18. There were sheds in the back. In the Wa-

Alice Sampson Home *(MDC Photo)*

ter Commission appraisal photographs, these two properties appear to be somewhat unkempt, with many objects lying in the yards. Perhaps some of these things were left behind when the families moved, as there are many bits of metal and other artifacts at these cellarholes.

The road to the right passes three cellarholes on its downhill route toward the shoreline. The Albert Sampson place is on the left, a few hundred feet east of George Sampson Jr.'s cellarhole. The home was set back from the road a bit; the cellarhole is mostly filled in. This was a 5 room, 1 1/2 story home, with a barn and henhouse. Earlier owners included L.J. Chamberlain, the Gee family (1880s), and George and Frank Sampson.

A bit further down on the left are the two open cellarholes of the Lillie Waterman place. Earlier owners included J. Page, then C. Bliss in the middle 1800s, and Betsey and Hartwell Crowl in the late 1800s. Waterman, a "soldier's widow," got it from Howard Joslyn (her father?) in 1917. Her son Fred was a minor league baseball pitcher.

This 1 1/2 story home had a large barn out back, a garage, and sheds across the road. Just before this road hits the shoreline, there is a road to the right. A lane off of this road to the right goes almost back to the Tupper cellarhole. The road to the right meets the old East Main St. at the crossroads at Vineca's, so a short loop hike back to Gate 26 is possible.

MAP OF GATES 26-7 AREA

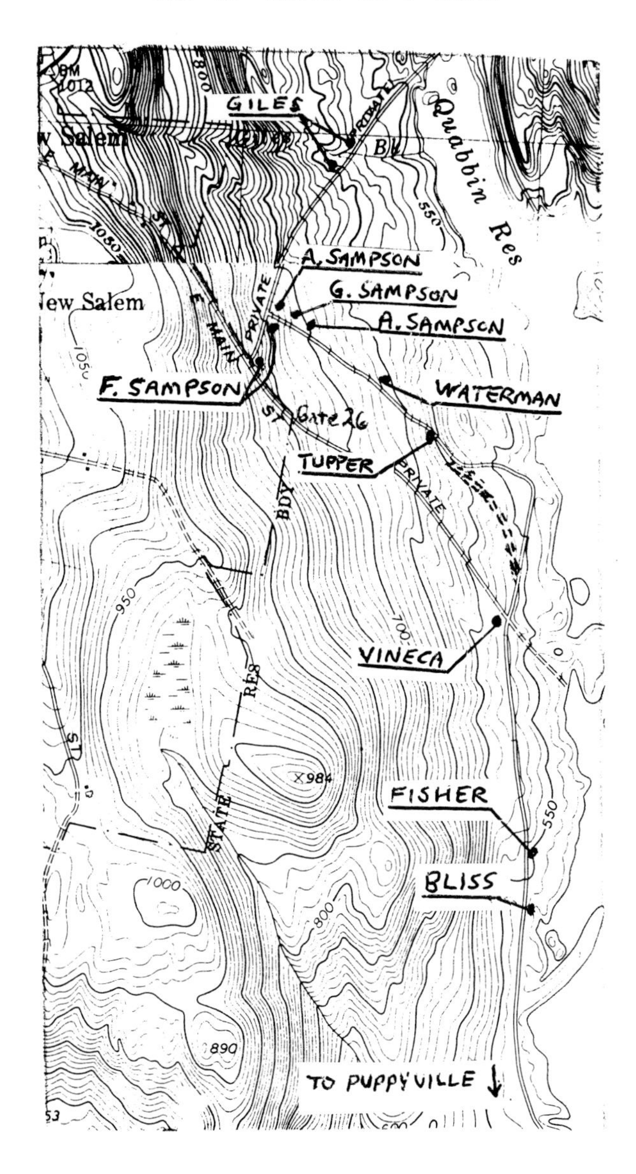

Chapter 10 - HERRICKS (Gates 29-30)

Gates 29 and 30 lead to the same road on the northern end of the reservation, so they will be covered in the same chapter. Gate 29 is an extenion of Elm St., which runs north of Route 202 toards North New Salem and Lake Mattawa in Orange. The Swift River Valley Historical Society museum complex is located on Elm St., about halfway to North New Salem, across from the Orange Oil Co. (See Chapter 23).

The road inside of Gate 29 is dirt, and runs through a stretch of piney woods. There are some numbered posts on the roadside; these mark an interpretive trail that was made in the mid-1980s. It was intended to explain some of the forest management practices in the reservation. A booklet detailing what these markers mean is available at the Quabbin Visitor's Center. An old wood road on the left comes out on the road from Gate 30.

Gate 30, a paved road, was originally the main road from Orange to Millington. There is a knoll to the right of the gate; this was the site of the Chandler home (A. Alden in 1870). The cellarhole of this 1 1/2 story home (with attached shed) was obliterated.

Once inside of the gate, look for the stone county highway marker on the right. Just past this is a marvel of construction known as the Keystone Bridge. A Millington man, Adolphus Porter, built it in 1866 by hand fitting the stones. It has held up almost perfectly in the intervening century and a third. The Y-shaped posts that are still on the bridge once held square wooden guardrails. The Middle Branch of the Swift River flows under this bridge; in the mid-1800s, a sawmill was located just downstream. The fact that this is a popular fishing spot is proven by the pathways that run along both sides of the river.

At the top of a small hill, on the right, is the obliterated Bert Terry cellarhole. This was a long, one story house, with sheds on the left side of the road. Captain Adams, who ran the sawmill below the bridge, lived here in 1870.

After a corner. the road follows a relatively straight course before it joins the road from

Gate 29. There was a home inside the Y of the junction after the Civil War, but it was a cellarhole before the reservoir came.

Just after the junction, there are fields on both sides of the road that were reclaimed in the late 1980s. A few birdhouses have been placed here. There are many old sugar maple trees lining the road in this section.

There are obliterated cellarholes on both sides of the road here. These were part of the 120 acre farm of Mary Davenport (W. Gill's in 1870). She was one of the survivors of the sinking of the ferryboat "City of Boston" in March, 1904. The stairway from this house was moved to a home in Williamstown. She died in New Salem in 1932.

There was another home not far down the road; the double barn cellarhole is visible on the left. Just north of a crossroads, this 122 acre farm was A. W. Lynde's in 1871; Per Applequist bought it in 1906. The 2 1/2 story,10 room house, on the right side of the road, had a small entry porch, and a two story ell. There was a double barn across the street. When the Water Commission went to appraise the property, they offered much less than the Applequist's asking price of $21,000! The Applequists celebrated their 40th wedding anniversary here in 1935. This house was reportedly rebuilt in Williamstown, Mass.

At the crossroads, the road on the left leads eastward to the boat launch ramp at Fishing Area

Applequist's Barn ***(MDC Photo)***

#2 (Gate 31), which provides a loop hike if one doesn't mind walking along Route 122 for the last third of the route back to Gate 30. A road that runs to the right off this one just east of the crossroads is a dead end in the woods; the Carpenter farm was located there in the late 1800s.

Where the road to the east originally crossed the Swift River at a site just below the present horseshoe dam was a mill with a canal. This section was jokingly referred to as New Buffalo, from an old story. Florence C. Cox relates that some boys were going to go to Buffalo, N.Y. to pick hops. Apparently, they bought some liquor, got drunk, and hid out here for a day or two. After it was learned that they never made the trip, the nickname was given to this section.

The road to the right, which is lined with maples, takes a hilly course through the woods to the west. There is only one cellarhole on this road, which passes under power lines near a ledge that can be seen from Route 202. It eventually joins up with the road from Gate 28, which in turn comes back to our paved road further down.

Continuing straight down the paved road, it passes over a buried telephone line. There is a nice tree-lined straight stretch here; the 1870 B. A. Bachelor home on the left was a cellarhole before the coming of the reservoir. Shortly after this, the road passes under power transmission lines.

Just after the lines, on the right at the edge of a reclaimed field, is an open cellarhole. This was the seven room home of Mary Aldrich; it was owned by Mrs. S. Wheeler in 1870. There is a pine grove on the left as the road gradually ascends a small hill. At the hilltop is the road junction, known for many years as Herricks.

A tavern was built on the northwest corner of this junction in the 1830s; one of the original owners was Captain Daniel Putnam. Later, it was known as the Whittemore Tavern. Before the Civil War, there was a post office here, and it was a stop for stagecoaches passing between Worcester and Brattleboro or Greenfield. When Moses Herrick (from Holliston) bought this around the Civil War, it was renamed for him. His son Howard resided there until his death in 1898.

Succeeding owners included R. T. Shumway, who renovated the place, and William Ward, who catered to groups of travelers. Solomon Converse occupied the building as a home when it burned down in a September, 1912 fire. A smaller home was later built on the site by Robert Bullard, who moved out in 1939. The house Bullard built here was removed to Athol.

Herrick's Tavern

The cellarholes of two barns are visible across the road east of the tavern. A chapter of the Telephone Pioneers of America erected a sign in the mid-1980s to mark the site of this tavern.

The road to the left at this junction goes eastward through the woods a for less than a mile to come out at a nice vista along the shore of one of the northern arms of the reservoir.

Turning right along the paved road, the cellarholes of the Howard Crowl home (D. Whitaker in the 1850s) and barn are on the left.

The partly discernable cellarhole of the Baines home is next, on the right side of the road; T. Putnam lived here in the 1850s. This was a six room house, which the couple bought in 1928, probably never suspecting the Water Commission would want to own it a few years later!

Just beyond this on the right was the site of the old District School #7.. This closed in 1902, reopened briefly, then closed again for good, the building being sold off.

Not far down the paved road, the dirt road from Gate 28 comes in from the right, making a Y-type junction. To do a loop, take this road, and a right off of it before the gate, to return to "New Buffalo" four corners.

After this "Y," the paved road rounds a corner, and begins to drop down hill, crossing over a brook. There is a fork in the road here. The dirt road to the right (sometimes called Beldin Hill Road) crosses a causeway over a bay in the reservoir (formerly Moosehorn Brook). The points of interest there are covered in Chapter 9.

The paved road to the left continues along a ridge overlooking this reservoir bay for a third of a mile before sloping down a short hill into the reservoir.

Near the top of this slope, there are several cellarholes on the left. The one closest to the road was known as the Webster place, last owned by William Davenport. The one behind that was the Fleck home, a 2 1/2 story building with ells, and a couple of barns in the back. These homes were owned by two Haskells in the 1870s. The house cellarholes are both constructed with intricately fitted together stones, with foundations larger than the cellars.

The road re-emerges onto the island south of where it enters the reservoir, but it disappears again after a short distance.

Webster and Fleck Homes

MAP OF GATES 29-30 AREA

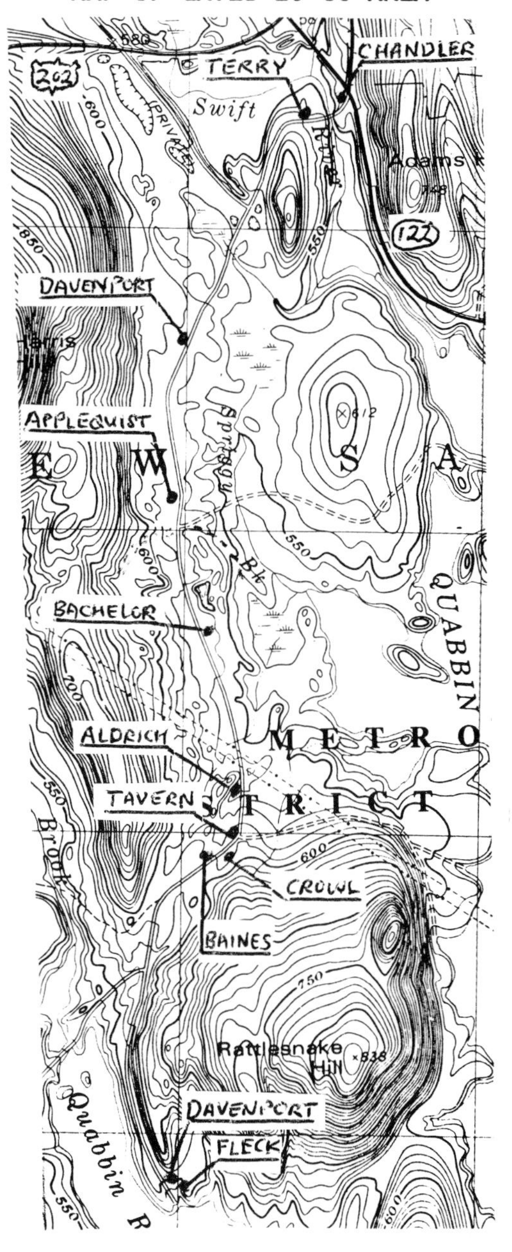

Chapter 11 - HACKER POND (Gate 33)

The roads leading in from Gates 33 and 35 connect not far from the reservoir shoreline, so they will be covered in the same chapter. They also provide the potential for at least three loop hikes varying from short to quite long distances. Gate 33 (or the Blackinton Road) also has two of the more fascinating building ruins in the northern part of the reservation.

To reach Gate 33, go on Route 122 between Routes 202 and 32. About a half mile west of the junction of Route 122 with the South Athol Road is a flat stretch of highway (west of the Spectacle Ponds), with a dirt road on either side of it. The road to the north is Blackinton Road, which is a back route to South Athol or Orange. The road on the south side of the highway is where Gate 33 is located.

Park next to the gate. You will find this a fairly level road for most of its length. The woods along it are rather piney, and there are swamps on the left. After about a half mile, you will come to a junction of four roads, and see the pond off to the left. In the 1850s, W. Smith lived on the southwest side of this crossroads; it was a cellarhole before the reservoir came.

The road to the left goes through Gate 34, coming out at the South Athol - North Dana Road at the hamlet of Hagerville. The road to the right goes up over Bassett Hill. At the top of the hill is a crossroads. The road to the left goes down (past the 1800s Bassett cellarhole on the right) to rejoin the road from Gate 33. The road to the right ends up at Gate 32, on Route 122. This gate wasn't properly marked until 1992.

Continue straight through the crossroads, and you will soon come to a Y in the road. The road to the left goes down a hill into the water. If you walk along the shoreline a short distance, you will come upon a shack. It was once used by the power company crews to store a boat, which enabled them to get to their transmission towers on a nearby island. If you take a right at the Y, you will eventually reach (over an M.D.C.-made road) Fishing Area #2. This would enable you to make a loop hike via the paved Gate 31 road and along Route 122 back to your starting point.

Returning to the crossroads at the pond, turn right (or go straight through, if you did not go up Bassett Hill), which goes along the west shore of the pond. This pond has several names. On the 1795 map of New Salem, it is named Hagar Pond. When one Bassett owned a mill near here, it was called Bassett Pond. Two 1800s maps call it Hacker Pond. There are some high-bush blueberry bushes along the shore of this shallow pond. Soon after the road veers away from the shoreline, go into the woods on the left. There are the cellarholes of Harry Hackett's 270 acre camp complex.

The buildings here included a cabin, camp, and garage built of logs, an ice house, and a laundry. A well-built stone chimney, with its fireplace, and foundation walls mark the main cabin site. Hackett had a fine view of the pond he owned from the back porch. Two different people bought these buildings in 1944 for $350.00, and moved them to Lake Wickaboag in West Brookfield.

Hackett's Camp *(MDC Photo)*

Going back on the road, there is a woodsy section. Note the rusted remains of an old car on the left. The road from Gate 32 joins this road on the right. The way continues level through a woodsy stretch, with an open section visible in the distance. As you approach the open stretch, look on the left for a small opening in the woods, with a few stones that appear to be marking an entrance to something.

If you are standing at the former entrance to this site, there is what appears to be a small low-lying cave at the rear of the clearing. This was the Golden Lake Cemetery; the "cave" is the remnant of the crypt. All of the 177 graves from this cemetery were removed to the Quabbin Park Cemetery in Ware.

Returning to the road, and continuing southward, the open area is revealed to be caused by the power lines passing overhead. There are several cellarholes under the power lines on the left, near a road junction. This was the Arthur Davis residence (B. Smith in the mid-1800s); which had three barns. The wellhead is still evident.

At the junction, the paved road is old Route 21, the South Athol - North Dana Rd. The road to the right quickly goes down to the waterline. At that point, if you wish to go to the railroad bed (visible on the opposite shoreline to your left) follow the path to the left through the woods above the flowline. After crossing a causeway, you will reach the cindered railroad bed.

If you turn left onto the paved road at the powerlines, it will lead you to Gate 35. A loop is possible walking the short distance to the Gate, then following the road for a half-mile north (past two houses), then taking a left at the little used road behind the long white house at Hagerville four corners. That road goes through Gate 34 back to the crossroads by Hacker Pond.

MAP OF GATES 33-36

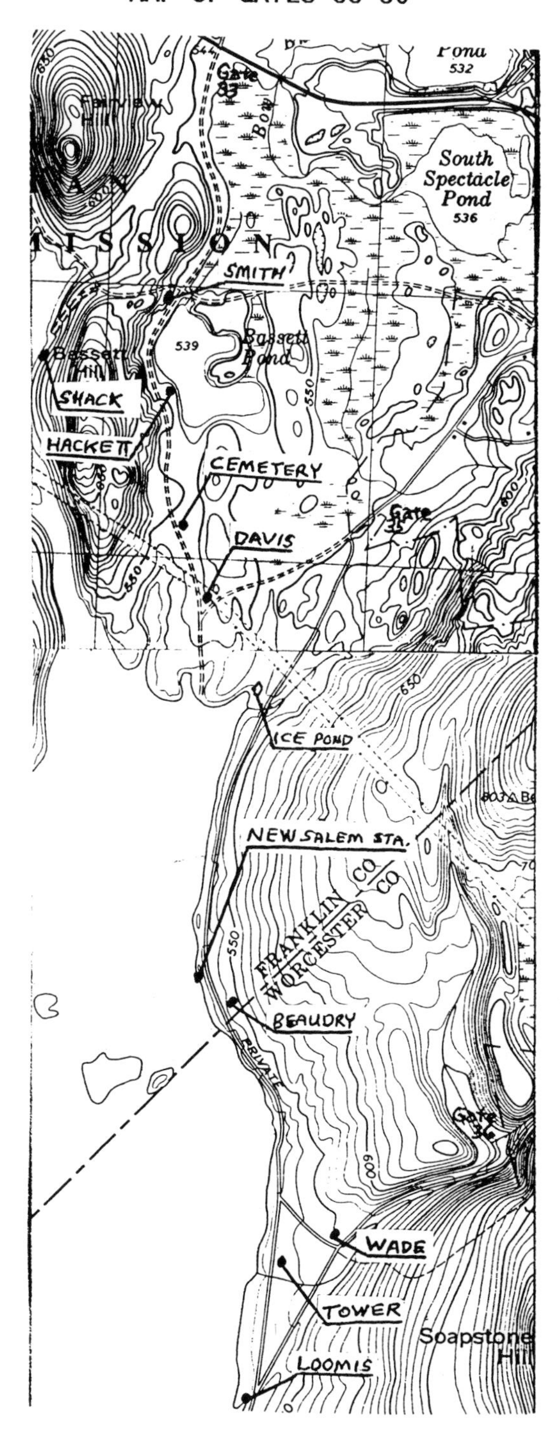

Chapter 12 - RAILROAD BED (Gate 35)

Gate 35 is on old Route 21, which connected Athol with Belchertown before the reservoir flooded the valley. This can be reached by turning south off Route 122 onto the South Athol - North Dana Rd. The part of the road that heads north toward South Athol is a few hundred feet west on the opposite side of the road from this turn.

On its way to the gate, the road passes through the four corners at the hamlet of Hagerville. There is a dirt road crossing past the volunteer fire station; the right leads to Gate 34 and Hacker Pond. Continuing down the paved road, it passes a farmhouse to the left on a sharp corner, then parallels the old railroad bed past two homes and a lumber yard, before crossing over the bed. When the railroad tracks were torn up in 1935, the ties were left in the roadway, which make it very rough to drive over!

There are parking spots before the gate and to the right of it. A path runs around it to the left, or you can walk around the gate itself. The paved road heads south for a half-mile or so to the junction with the road from Gate 33 at the power lines (see Chapter 11).

If you take a left just inside the gate, you will soon come upon the railroad bed. Unlike the Mass. Central project described in Chapter 21, this was a functioning railroad for six decades. Built in the early 1870s as the Athol & Enfield RR, it later became the Athol Branch of the Boston & Albany RR. The Water Commission purchased the railroad above Bondsville in 1935, and the tracks were torn up that summer. Most of the old bed back to Athol can still be found, although much of it is on private property.

The first stretch of the railroad bed inside of Gate 35 runs through a wooded area, much of which is higher than the level of bed. It is a cool hike in the summer months. The shade ends where the power transmission lines pass over the bed, just before it reaches the reservoir shoreline.

Just past the power lines, a look to the right will reveal what looks like a beaver pond. This was originally Goodnow's ice pond. In the time before refrigeration, people would cut ice from ponds during the winter, and store it in sawdust in specially built sheds, until it was used during the warm months of the year.

There is a path down from the railroad bed, along the top of the ice pond dam, and along the shoreline to the left. This joins up with the road from Gate 35, for a short loop hike.

The Goodnow home is a cellarhole only a few dozen feet out from the shoreline off the railroad bed; it is visible only during low water periods.

Shortly after this pond, a large section of land off the the right was used as a sand pit in the 1980s. Then the railroad bed follows the shoreline for about a half mile. There are several well-preserved stone culverts on this stretch; some are popular spots for shore fishermen.

After passing by a small hillock on the shore side, the railroad bed becomes a sandy road, curving off toward the left. The railroad bed may be discerned as a depression in the ground to the right, along the shore. If you step off the road, and follow this to the sandy shoreline, you may find the remnants of the foundation of the old New Salem railroad station. This station building was rebuilt on Rte. 202 in New Salem; and is now called "Millington Crossing."

New Salem Railroad Station

When the water is a bit low, you can also make out parts of two paved roads that joined here.

One connected the station with Milington village; the other, which emerges from the water onto a point of land, is old Route 21.

Since Route 21 reemerges further down the shoreline, it was deemed expedient to build a dirt road to connect it with the end of the railroad bed. Just before going over a small hill, beside a point of land jutting out into the reservoir, a "witness marker" stone is on the side of the road away from the shore. This indicates the boundary between New Salem and Petersham, which is also a county boundary.

Just before the witness marker, there is a clearing on the left. The cellarhole of the Alfred Beaudry place is about 150 feet in from the shore. There was a barn, and several sheds on the property.

After passing over the small hill, you can look toward the shoreline when the water level is down a bit, and spot broken tar pieces from old Route 21 along the shoreline. At a short curve, where a small brook runs through a culvert, this dirt road joins the paved road which reemerges from the shoreline.

There are two stone posts next to the road along the shore here. These were on the property of Fred Gannon. Offshore is the site of the home of Mabel Beebe, which was the only Petersham home inundated by the reservoir.

A short distance beyond the Beebe site is a dirt road off to the left. This is the upper arm of a right-facing triangle of roads. Less than a quarter-mile down this left is a junction with the road from Gate 36 at a large beaver pond. On the northwest side of this junction was the Nancy Wade farm (L.Sibley's in 1870; L. G. Bassett's in 1898). The large barn cellarhole is at the end of a stonewall-lined driveway. The open house cellarhole faces the Gate 36 road.

A loop hike back to Route 122 via. Gate 36 and the North Dana Road to Gate 35 is about 4 1/2 miles. There are a couple of cellarholes on the north side of the road to Gate 36 east of Wade's.

The road to the right at the beaver pond returns to the paved road; it is often flooded in the spring.

Continuing down the paved road from just past the Beebe place, one should look near the base of a large tree on a small knoll to the left for an old stone post. A "P" was cut into one side, and a "D" into the other. This marked the boundary between Petersham and Dana at this point. Across from this are signs of gravel excavations.

Just beyond this is a clearing on the left, with a metal tower standing next to a small building. This was used for fire spotting in the past, but the removal of the lower sections of the stairs indicate that it has fallen into disuse.

If you look out over the water from this point along the shoreline, you may spot stretches of reeds sticking out of the water north of hilly Mt. L Island. The reeds are on rims of craters that were created when the reservoir was used for bombing practice during World War II. Anyone flying over this part of the reservoir (particularly during low water periods) can easily spot the craters.

A brook passes under the road just past the tower; this flows from the beaver pond mentioned six paragraphs ago. Then the road that forms the southeast arm of the road triangle comes in from the left in a attractive grove of pines. 150 feet past the junction, on the right, was the Charles W. Loomis place, a fine 2 1/2 story Victorian home, with an ell in back. The cellarhole is nearly obliterated.

Loomis Home

This was the O. Town(e) home in the 1850s, G. Winslow's (1870), and Mrs. Mary Bassett's (1898). Charles Loomis was the No. Dana correspondent for the *Barre Gazette* around 1920. The Loomis family relocated to Somers, CT.

Before the coming of the reservoir, the John Phillips family operated a tea room in the nearby village of Millington. When this burned in the 1920s, they moved the business here, renting the place from the Water Commission. The ell was used for the tea room. This was operated into the 1930s, until the family had to move out. One can imagine that much of the tea room's business must have come from the curious driving along Route 21 to visit the dying valley.

Upon leaving the grove, the road proceeds a-round a gentle curve to the left, then follows a straight course along the shoreline for close to a half mile. Near the end of this stretch, a dirt road veers off to the left up a hill. This is an M.D.C.- built road up over Soapstone Hill. This comes from the road from Gate 37 (mentioned in Chapter 13). A loop hike of over six miles can be done via Gate 37 and the old Monson Turnpike Road back up to Route 122 and the North Dana Road to Gate 35. If you climb up Soapstone hill over the road, head south through the woods at the peak. There are some magnificent views of the reservoir from the top of Soapstone Hill. Depending upon where you end up, you may have to climb a tree to see anything!

Shortly after passing the Soapstone Hill access road, old Route 21 goes into the water at a reedy place on the shoreline. This is about a mile north of the site of North Dana (see Chapter 13). There is a nice view here (toward the southwest) of the gap between Mt. Zion and Mt. L islands.

Chapter 13 - NORTH DANA (Gate 37)

North Dana was the major factory village of the town of Dana. Due to its being located on the Middle Branch of the Swift River, most of the village was flooded by the reservoir. During periods of low water, parts of it reappear in the form of streets, ornamental walls, and a few cellarholes.

One street of the village is still above the waterline, at the tip of a peninsula that juts southward from Soapstone Hill. To hike to this area, one can follow the shoreline from the end of roads that reach the northern edge of this peninsula. The west side approach is from the end of the road from Gates 35 or 36. This is a tougher hike, and swampy in places at high water.

The easier (and more interesting) approach to North Dana is from the east. This is reached from Gate 37, which is on the old Monson Turnpike Road, off West St. in Petersham.

This turnpike, like the one at Gate 11 in Pelham, was built by a corporation chartered by the state. Begun in 1804 as the Petersham and Monson Turnpike, it ran southward from Athol through Petersham, Dana, Greenwich, Enfield, Ware, Palmer, and Monson to Stafford Springs, Ct.

The cellarhole before the gate was the O. Amsden place in 1870, and George Kendall's in 1898. The one at the gate was A. Spooner's in 1870, and E. Ward's in 1898. Both of these farms were gone before the reservoir came. Not far inside of the gate. there is a roadstone marking the original boundary between Dana and Petersham.

Follow this road down the hill, to the bridge over the West Branch of Fever Brook. The road is paved just before and after the bridge. A left before the bridge leads to the site of Doubleday Village (See Chapter 14).

The cellarholes on the southwest and southeast sides of this junction belonged to Myron and Elvie Doubleday. The 1 1/2 story cape was at the open cellarhole on the left just before the bridge. The barn cellarhole on the left is mostly filled in. This was the L. B. Williams place in the late 1800s.

After crossing the bridge, there is an open celarhole on the right. This was a 7 room, 1 1/2 story home, last owned by Joseph Piette. A Mrs. Blackmour owned this in 1870, Edward Tyler in 1898, and Clara King before 1916.

The original paved turnpike road veers off to the left, and into the water. There is an open cellarhole on the left before the shoreline; this was home of Rosa and Lillian Dowd. Charles F. Tollman owned this 1 1/2 story, 4 room home in 1870; Angelica Horr in 1898, and Napoleon Chelifoux from 1908-18.

Follow the dirt road that bears right from the paved road. This M.D.C. - made road goes around a small bay in the reservoir. Just as the road begins to head up a hill away from the bay, a dirt road is on the left. Take this left, which passes by an interesting cellarhole. This was the Katie Whipple place (L. Doubleday's in 1898). A widow, she took in laundry to support herself.

Katie Whipple's *(MDC Photo)*

Across from this cellarhole was the site of the bedstead with a tree grown through it used on the front cover of this book.

When you reach the shoreline, turn right and follow it through the woods. When the water level is low, you can follow the roadway of the old Monson Turnpike for part of the way. Part of the old L. Doubleday farm is visible where the road briefly emerges from the water at one point.

As you approach the site of No. Dana, you will pass the remains of a couple of concrete platforms overlooking the water. These were built for gunnery practice and observation during World War II. Since the reservation was unoccupied, and the area south and east of these platforms was quite flat and open, it was ideal for small arms and aerial bombing practice. Warplanes flying out of Westover Air Force Base in Chicopee were allowed to drop real and dummy bombs there (and in Prescott). The results could be easily observed from these platforms.

There are several ledges as one rounds a point turning westward along the shoreline. During low water, rusted bits of metal and pieces of broken glass in the sand remind the visitor that people once lived here. Just west of where a brook flows into the reservoir, pieces of lead pipe can be seen. These were from a well up on the hill, which can still be found. It served as a water supply for some of the homes in North Dana.

There are three cellarholes on the hilltop west of the wellhead. The one furthest north, at the end of the Lorenzo Hale Road, was the Ella Higgins (earlier Hale) home.

Another cellarhole is located on the west side of this peninsula, not far above the waterline; this was the two story Edward Rohan place. It, and a nearby barn were torn down in 1929.

Part of No. Dana facing East (Rohan house at top, bandstand at bottom)

A cellarhole down near the waterline, on the east side of the old street, was owned by Irene Marc Aurele after 1920 (Munroe Snow in 1898). It was a 1 1/2 story, 7 room home with a porch added by Marc Aurele. In the late 1920s, a music teacher who came to the village to give piano lessons would use the Marc Aurele's piano. When the family sold out, her son Malcolm Marc Aurele ran a food store in Athol. In 1931, Frank Witt of Amherst bought this place from the Water Commission, and moved it away.

A sloping ledge sticks out into the water just west of here. Since this is just above the site of the village Methodist Church, some call this Methodist Point. This church, one of three in the village, was one of the last buildings torn down there in 1939.

North Dana Methodist Church

One other sign of civilization can still be found on this point; there are a couple of power transmission poles! These are not remnants of North Dana, but were part of a line strung into the area to provide power for logging operations during the lowest water period in the mid-1960s.

Chapter 14 - DOUBLEDAY VILLAGE

This hamlet was located on the East Branch of Fever Brook. At least two sawmills operated here for several decades. Joseph Doubleday started this business in the 1820s. Joseph's decendants ran sawmills until the late 1800s. Samuel Whiting ran a sawmill and box shop here for several years until it burned in 1909.

At one time almost all of the residents of the hamlet were Doubledays, giving the place its name. Sometimes it was called Doubledayville. Records from the 1850 Federal Census indicate that 9 of the 15 adult Doubledays in the state resided in Dana.

The site of this hamlet is just above the waterline. It is most easily reached from the roads at Gate 37, or Gate 38. Another possible approach is from Gate 39, which is on the Dugway Rd. (off Route 32A) in Petersham. Roads from Gates 38 and 39 lead to the northern ends of the Tamplin and Whitney Hill Roads, mentioned in the Chapters 16-17.

To get to Doubleday Village from Gate 37, follow the road in from the gate down to where it crosses the West Branch of Fever Brook. Just before the bridge, there is a road off to the left. Go down this road for about 3/5 of a mile, until you reach an angled crossroads. The road on the immediate right goes back to the shoreline. The second right goes down to the west side of Doubleday Village. This grassy road passes a swamp on the left, and the ledges of Rattlesnake Hill on the right on its 1 1/4 mile route.

Just after the ledges, there is a cellarhole in a walled-in lot on the left. This was the P. Coval farm in the 1850s, but it was gone long before the reservoir came.

As you approach the village site, there will be a swamp on the left, which was the old mill pond. The road shortly takes a turn to the left, onto an old bridge abutment; this is the west side of Doubleday Village.

Remains of the old dam can still be seen where Fever Brook flows out of the swamp above the abutment. There are a few sections of walls and scattered bricks on this side of the stream to mark the site of one of the Doubleday sawmills. This was last operated by E. F. Bristol around 1900. The bridge that was here was removed when the reservoir came, so that you will have to "jump stones" near the dam to cross Fever Brook.

To walk to the east side of Doubleday Village from the last mentioned road junction, bear directly left. This road passes by an area logged off around 1990; it was Thomas Hanafin's Sunnyside Farm. There are open cellarholes on the left a few hundred feet east of the junction. This was a 1 1/2 story 10 room home, with a shed and barn attached. Earlier owners included J. Witt (middle 1800s), Z.B. Powell (1898), David Kennedy, and Guy Stevens. There is a well with stone slabs covering it in front of the cellarholes.

Thomas Hanafin's *(MDC Photo)*

Just east of the Hanafin cellarholes is an old field surrounded by electric fencing. This is one of several areas in the Quabbin Reservation that has been set up to see if this method will keep out deer, who would otherwise eat young saplings.

The eastern edge of the fenced-in area borders an old lane. The longtime home of Frederick Foster was located on the northeast side of the junction. The open cellarhole was the site of a small 1 1/2 story home.

Take the right here, crossing over the East Branch of Fever Brook. An old millsite is discernible just above the bridge; there is a swamp downstream. The next junction is with the road from Gate 38. Take the road to the right at the junction to reach Doubleday Village.

There is a cellarhole on the southwest side of this junction. It was part of a farm owned by one Amsden in the 1850s, C. Gleason in 1870, and A. B. Knapp in 1898. An old cellarhole next to a large wall not far south of here was part of the same farm. The buildings were gone before the reservoir came.

This road junction can be reached from Gates 38 or 39. To come in from Gate 39, take the Dugway Road off Rte. 32A in southern Petersham. Park at the gate, then take the first right, not far inside the gate. At the junction a third of a mile from the first turn, take a left onto the road from Gate 38, and follow the directions from there stated in the next paragraph.

Gate 38 is on the Camel's Hump Rd., which is reached from West St. in Petersham. There is a cemetery on the left where Camels Hump Rd. meets West St. Just before the gate, there is a stone marker post for the old boundary between Dana and Petersham.

A bit less than a mile in from the gate, there is a fork in the road at the old Wesley and Myra Ploof cellarhole (W. Kendall's in 1870). This was a 2 1/2 story house, with a barn past it. Just before this junction, on the right, is the site of the Williams Cemetery, which held 55 graves.

Take your right at the junction, which passes by the Peter and Roseanna Pluff house and barn cellarhole on the left. This 1 1/2 story home (C. Gleason's in 1870) had several sheds on the property. Pluff ran a milk route for many years. When they sold out in the late 1920s, the Pluffs moved to Grafton, which had been their home before coming to Dana around 1898.

In a half mile, there is another junction. The site of an old district school (later a house) is on the left here; take the road to the right.

Another road junction follows shortly; the road to the right is the one from Gate 37 described earlier. The road to the left will take you to the east side of Doubleday Village.

There were two farmsteads on this stone wall-lined road north of Doubleday Village. The first one was the Henrietta Allen place. The barn is the first cellarhole, then the open one of the 2 1/2 story house, both on the right. This was owned by Moses Knapp's family in the 1800s. Knapp (1840-1929) was active in town government for many years, including serving as a selectman. In the time around World War I, some of the locals called this the "haunted house." The Olaf Olafson family was the last to live here. When her husband died, Mrs. Olafson married Gustaf Soderberg, an Athol man.

The next place was located at breaks in the stone walls on both sides of the road. The last owner by Kristine Olsen. There was barn on the right; the filled-in cellarhole of the 1 1/2 story cape-style house is on a knoll at the left. There was a barn and sheds in the back. A brick-yard on this property in the 1800s was run by Jacob Amsden; it was the source of bricks for the Joseph Doubleday home mentioned below.

Earlier owners of this farm were E. Davis in 1857, William Chamberlain in 1870, and Horace Wood (from 1881 to 1918), After a brief ownership by the Burbees, the place was bought in late 1918 by Anton Olsen, a native of Norway.

Olsen had been a mechanic in the Brooklyn Navy Yard during World War I. He raised poultry here until his death in 1937. Ironically, his son Tony worked as a mechanic on New York City's Delaware River Water Supply project. After selling out, Mrs. Olsen moved to Hardwick.

The beginning of Doubleday Village proper is marked by cellarholes at breaks in the stonewalls lining both sides of the road. The filled-in cellarhole on a knoll to the left was the home of Wilfred and Helen Lyman from 1921. He ran an ice business from this village. It was a 1 1/2 story 10 room home, with a bay window over a porch. Part of the barn cellarhole in back is visible; there were also several sheds. Earlier owners included O.N.Doubleday (mid-1800s), Charles Hale, Charles Goodman, and Albert Alberta (1897-1902).

The partially filled-in cellarhole on the right was the Jennie Bishop home. Moving here in 1899,

Lyman Home

(with her husband Fred) she was the last decendant of Joseph Doubleday living in the village at its demise; she relocated to Orange. This two-section 1 1/2 story house had a barn and sheds in back. Earlier owners were J.F. Chamberlin in 1873, C. H. Briggs, and J. E. Doubleday.

The next house was about 200 feet down the road on the left, at a break in the stone wall just before a road junction. This was the 1 1/2 story farm of Dominick Dumas. This long house ran back from the street to a barn; there were also several sheds. The cellarhole is filled in. Dumas' son Ray was a wellknown musician in Athol for many years. The Oscar Anderson family (he was a cousin of Emil Malm) rented this place from Dumas for several years before it was sold to the Water Commission. Earlier owners were Nehemiah Doubleday (Joseph's son) in the mid-1800s, and Austin Lewis in 1898. According to Grace Oakes, several of the large maple trees here were planted by Nehemiah Doubleday and Edward Goodman in 1876.

Take a right at the road junction; the filled-in cellarhole on the right was the known as the brick house. This large 2 1/2 story home had a wooden ell on the right. Emil and Hilva Malm were the last owners (from 1918); they moved to Connecticut in 1927. Mrs. Malm often organized maypole dances and Christmas parties for the village children. The Soderbergs rented this from the Commission for several years, before it was demolished in the summer of 1936. A high wall across from the house marks the site of the barn.

Elkanah Doubleday Home

Joseph Doubleday built this home around 1824. His son J. Elkanah Doubleday (1838-1922) lived here for decades,before moving to North Dana. Elkanah served Dana as tax collector and selectmen.

The bridge past this place was taken out before the reservoir came. The old millrace between the dam and the bridge site is still discernible. This was the Doubleday sawmill for many years; it was later run by Frank Whitney, L. W. Blackmer, E. F. Bristol, and Samuel Whiting.

Returning to the main road, and continuing southward, there is a filled-in cellarhole on the left at a break in the stone wall. This 1 1/2 story 8 room home was the Anna Soderberg place. There was an ell and a barn in back. L. Cooley lived here in 1857, Isaac Caldwell in 1898.

The last house in the village was about 250 feet past Soderbergs, on the right, past a junction of two stone walls. The barn, ell, and the 1 1/2 story home of Michel Burati were all obliterated. Previous owners included A.V. Kent (1857), H. Priest (1870), and Horace and Sarah Lindsey (1898). Burati came from Rhode Island to be an engineer at the Crawford and Tyler mill in North Dana. After selling out, he moved his family to Springfield; two of his sons became lawyers. The road goes into the water not far below this site.

MAP OF NORTH DANA & DOUBLEDAY VILLAGE

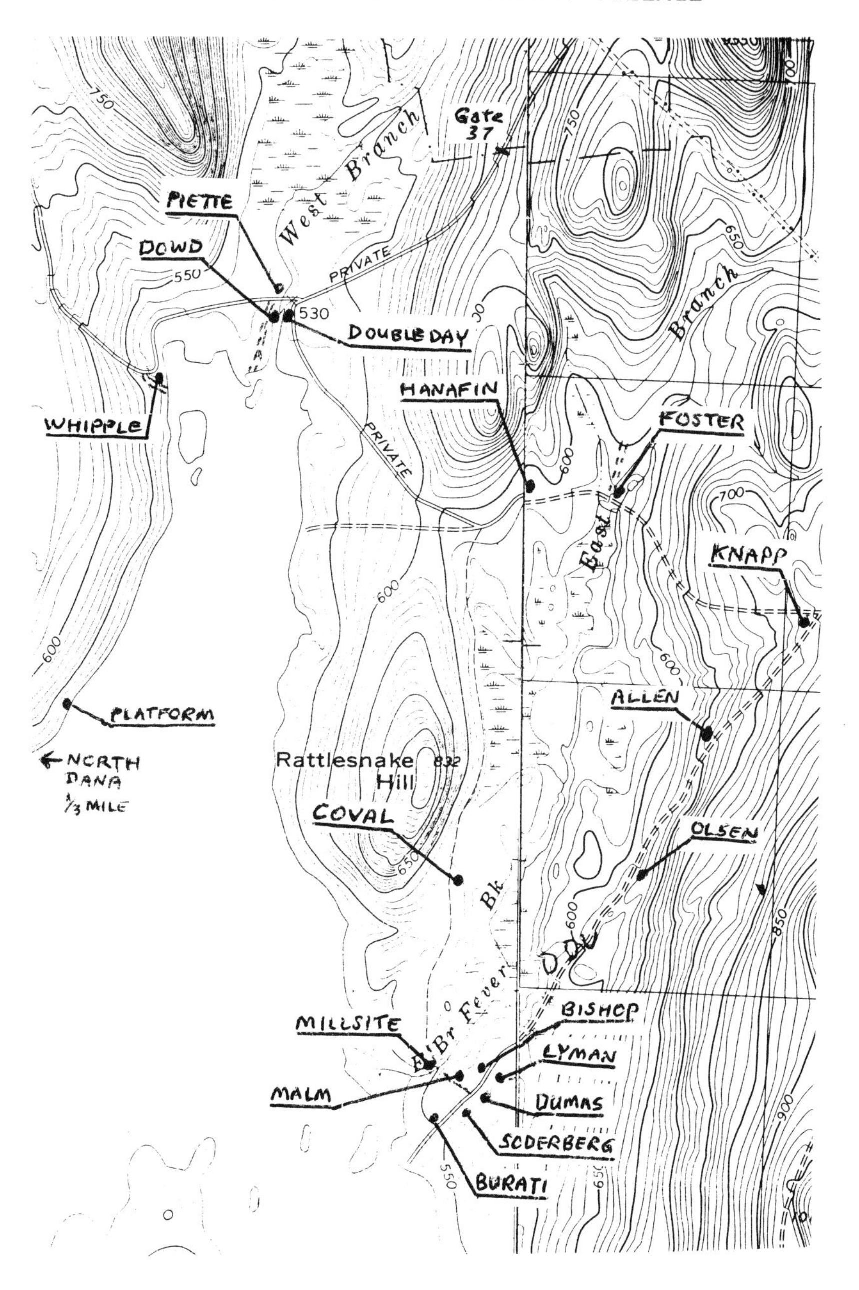

Chapter 15 - ROAD TO DANA COMMON (Gate 40)

This is by far the best "historical" hike in the Quabbin Reservation. The site of Dana Common village is the highlight of this hike, but there are several other points of interest in this section.

Gate 40 is located off Route 32A; 4 1/2 miles south of Route 122, or two miles north of the Petersham-Hardwick boundary sign. The gate is located in a hollow on the west side of the road. There are several parking spaces between Route 32A and the gate; these can be filled up during some weekends in the warmer months of the year.

Outside of the gate, you may note the remains of a road that seems to parallel Route 32A. This was the original roadway, before the present one was built to straighten out a sharp corner here.

The first sites of note in this section are outside of the gate. There is a nearly obliterated cellarhole in the woods on the right side of the road before the gate. Sheridan Hall was the last owner of this place; he had purchased it from Beatrice Miner in 1926. This was the home of Asa "Popcorn" Snow in the mid-1800s.

Home of "Popcorn Snow" *(MDC Photo)*

Snow led a rather odd and tragic life. Reportedly a vegetarian, he lived on a diet of milk and popcorn, hence the nickname. His first wife committed suicide by hanging herself in the barn in 1844. His young daughter died shortly afterward.

A daughter by his second wife had ten children, so Snow has many living decendants.

Snow is best remembered for the casket he had built for himself before he died. It was made of metal, which was unusual in that place and time; but what was even more unusual was the glass window placed over where his head would lay. He had this done so that he could be checked for seven days after his internment (in his own tomb) to be certain that he was dead.

Upon Snow's death, on November 29, 1872, he was laid to rest in the coffin, inside of the tomb. The undertaker went to the tomb for three days in a row to ensure that he was dead. When a bad snowstorm made it impossible for the man to get into the tomb, Snow's second wife released him from the obligation.

Snow's tomb was located in a cemetery behind the stone walls at the junction of the paved road and an old road at the top of the knoll just past the gate. This, like the other 150 known graves here, was removed to the Quabbin Park Cemetery in Ware, so no evidence of it is visible today.

(See Chapter 43 in the author's 1993 *"Strange Tales From Old Quabbin"* book for more on Snow.)

Snow had also owned the place that is an indistinct cellarhole on the left side of the road just outside of the gate. This was a two story mansard-roofed house. Nellie Dorow was the last owner; George Robbins lived here in 1898.

The two cellarholes and the cemetery just mentioned are within what has always been Petersham. The roadstone marking the boundary with Dana is beyond the end of a stone wall beside the road, not far past the old cemetery. When the four valley towns were disincorporated in 1938, all of the territory of Dana was absorbed by Petersham.

Continuing down the paved road, one will observe a small reclaimed field on the left, with birdhouses placed there. This, and several other plots along this road for the next mile and a half were planted with pines in the early 1940s. Many of these plots were logged off in the late 1980s, and restored to fields again.

A bit further along the way, there are reclaimed fields on both sides of the road, bordered by a brook. Part way along these are cellarholes on both sides of the road. The mostly filled-in one on the right has a large maple tree in front of it. This was the home of Monroe Berry, Dana's Animal Inspector in the 1920s.

Munroe Berry Farm *(MDC Photo)*

A sign on the barn identified this as Eastview Farm. A long ell ran along the road to connect the house with the barn, which was near the stone wall by the road. There is another barn cellarhole on the opposite side of the road. Before the Civil War, three Tolmans had homes here; in 1898 it was John Russell's. Myra Berry purchased this farm in 1901. In the winter of 1920, Berry's barn partly caved in from a heavy snowfall.

Down the road, just past an attractive brook, is a cellarhole partly visible on the left. This home was gone before the reservoir came. Opposite this was the Elizabeth McMaster house. A Springfield resident, she purchased this from Job Merriam in 1926. earlier owners included C. A. Stone in the middle 1800s, and Richard Fitzgerald in 1898. This home burned in 1928.

Just past here, the northeastern arm of the reservoir is visible through the trees on the left. An old oil tank at the edge of a field here may have been left behind by a timber salvage contractor cleaning up after the 1938 Hurricane.

The reclaimed fields on both sides of the road here were part of the George Carter farm. On the right side of the road, a large cellarhole is clearly visible; this was a large barn. A smaller, partly grown-in cellarhole just past it was the homestead. This was a large 2 1/2 story home, with an attached open ell. There was also a barn across the road, in the small clear spot.

George Carter Farm

From 1866-1921, this had been the town poor farm. The poor farm concept had been used in many New England communities as late as the 1940s for housing the poor and indigent. The "inmates" who were able were put to work raising crops, or doing small chores to help defray the town's cost of boarding them.

Among the wardens and matrons who operated the town poor farm were one Pierce (1876), Mr. and Mrs. William Shippee (of Barre) in the early 1880s, Amos T. Towne (who committed suicide there in 1887), Mr. and Mrs. Francis Simonds around 1890, Greenwich artist and photographer Burt V. Brooks (1891), one Pierce of Prescott (late 1890s), Mr. and Mrs. Berry (they received a $200.00 salary for 1899), Mr. and Mrs. Joseph Chelifoux (1914), and Melzar Bates at the end.

After the town no longer needed the place, the real estate and contents were sold off in early 1921. George Carter bought this for his use as a private farm. Walter Clark reported that Carter kept a flock of game birds here, and "sold many prize cockerels."

Shortly beyond this point there is a steep banking on the left side of the road for a distance, and ledges off to the right. Rounding a sharp corner, we come to the site of the farm of Ed and Lulu Spooner. E.G. Stone had owned this in the middle 1800s; Nathan Stone in 1898. The homestead was located on the walled-in knoll on the right. The cellarhole of the barn (there was also a shed) can be seen across the street to the left. When they sold out in 1931, the Spooners moved to a farm just a couple of miles to the east in Barre. Lulu died there five years later.

Spooner Home *(MDC Photo)*

After Spooner's, the road goes down a slight incline, with a field on the right, and stretch of pines on the left, (with a reclaimed field behind them). This leads up to a road junction. The land on the left, and on both sides of the road that comes in from the left was the farm of Daniel and Olean (Bosworth) LaPlante. The 11 room home, dating from about 1850, was located at the inside corner of the junction. In 1870, it was Stone and Comee's; in 1898 it was Bosworth's.

The LaPlantes moved to West Brookfield after selling out; Mrs.LaPlante died in December, 1936. George Southworth rented this place from the Water Commission in 1937; he removed to Warren.

A cement cellarhole for one of LaPlante's several farm buildings can be found east of the house site, in the pines previously mentioned, while the cellarholes of two barns are barely visible on the right after you turn onto the road that comes in from the left. In the view of the barn in this picture, note the old automobile parked behind the tree. That tree was still standing when this was written in 1994!

LaPlante's Barn *(MDC Photo)*

This road to the left is the old Barre-Dana Road. It was once paved, but only a few chunks of aspahlt remain to attest to that. This road goes downhill, past a pre-reservoir cellarhole on the right, which was the Tolman farm in 1870. Just below this is the site of the bridge over the East Branch of the Swift River. The approaches to the bridge are still evident. The one on this side is a popular fishing spot, due to the deep channel here.

Returning to the road to Dana, there is a large reclaimed field on the left, and what appears to be an old road on the right. The paved road was built as a bypass in the last years of the town to avoid the sharp curve on the old road.

After the old road rejoins the paved one, there is a stone wall along the right side of the road. The Margaret MacArthur home (and barn) was located behind the wall; it was nicknamed "Bonny Blink." Eariier owners were G. Charles in 1870, and the M. Gorman estate in 1898.

The cellarholes here are almost obliterated. MacArthur purchased this eight room house from

Margaret MacArthur Home

John Tyler in 1902, often using it as a summer home. When she sold it to the Water Commission, MacArthur told them the house dated from 1750, which may have been stretching out the age a bit! After selling out, she moved to Springfield.

Across the street from this one can see a large, rectangular stone, with a bolt sticking out of it. On the stone is the date 1899, and the letters "O A MARCILLE." This is all that remains of the first home of Dana's tragic blacksmith, Moses Marcille. Marcille and his family had lived here for seven years (it was the L. Doane place in the middle 1800s) when a fire burned the house down in 1899. Marcille moved to Fall River for awhile, but returned to Dana to live in a home just down the street. We will pick up his story there.

There is a swampy area on the left in a small hollow. A steam sawmill and wood shop was built here by S.E. and Z.W. Brown in 1855. This was operated by J.S. Brown until it burned in 1864. A small shop replaced this, which ended up as Marcille's, then Rollin Doubleday's blacksmith shop, then Les Cooley's garage.

On the right side of the road is the site of the John and Bertha Price home. This peak-roofed two story home had six rooms. There were two huge trees in front of the covered doorway. Price, from Springfield, bought this from George Warren in 1926. earlier owners included P. Williams in the middle 1800s, and Washington Robbins in 1898.

Price moved to Bondsville after selling out.

Price Home

As you head up the incline, Brown's Cemetery ran back from the road on the right. This 1 1/3 acre burial ground had 124 graves in it. The Dana Center cemetery was to the west of this, behind the town hall and school. You are now at the eastern edge of Dana Common, which will be described in the next chapter.

MAP OF ROAD TO DANA COMMON

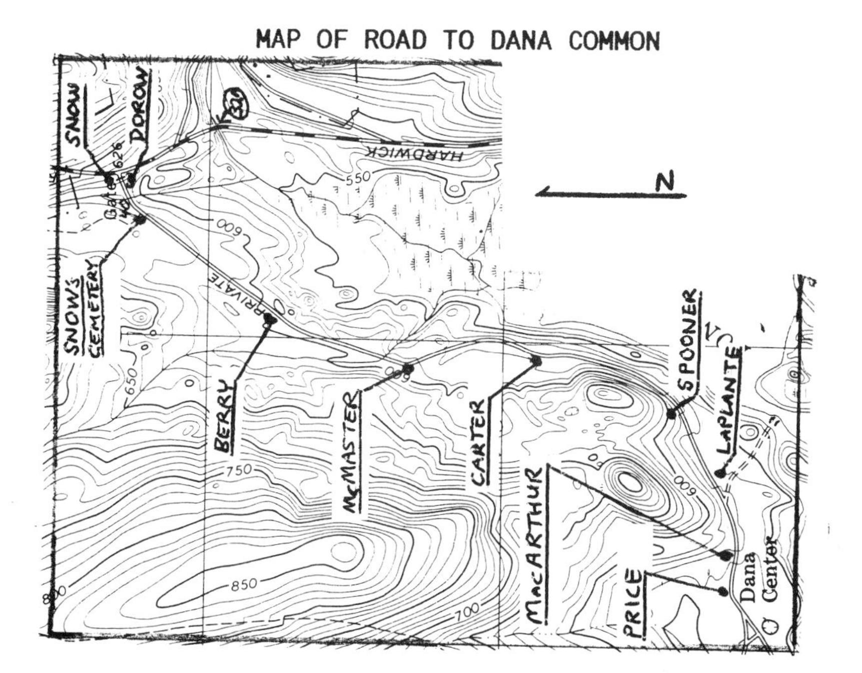

Chapter 16 - DANA COMMON

The sites and cellarholes of Dana Common will be followed in a counterclockwise fashion, from northeast to southeast.

Just west of the Price cellarhole is a grassed-in embankment that goes up from the paved road. Follow this along a stone wall here up to the top of the knoll, then turn right. The filled-in cellarhole, with a cement walkway leading up to it was the town hall.

This building was originally a Baptist church in the southern part of Petersham. The parish moved it to Dana around 1800, but disbanded by 1830. The town bought the building in 1842 to use for their town hall. The building was also being used for the village school when it was damaged by a fire in 1867; repairs were made a year later.

The town hall was slightly damaged by a fire in December,1877. A 16 year old boy was charged with setting the blaze, but was released due to insufficient evidence. When the town's property was auctioned off in 1938, this building brought $90.00, presumably for the lumber.

Dana School and Town Hall

To the left of the town hall was the village schoolhouse. The gaping cellarhole of this 2 1/2 story building is easy to find; keep a sharp eye out for it if you have young children with you! This was originally a one story building; the upstairs was added in 1892. A small room housed the village library. This brought $110.00 when it was sold off in the 1938 auction of Dana's property.

Students in grades one through eight were taught here; high schoolers had to go out of town. Did a teacher ever punish a naughty child by making him or her look out the back window at the cemetery grave monuments?

The eleven stone posts running to the left of the school cellarhole are the remnants of the southern boundary fence of the Dana Center Cemetery. There were 714 graves on this 2 1/3 acre site. This land was logged off around 1990, and reclaimed as a field. Some of the old tomb foundation stones are piled up near the town hall cellarhole.

Walking along the right side of the street on the north side of the common, parts of the old sidewalk will be encountered. When you come to a junction with a dirt road on the right, look behind the bushes until you spot the remains of a cellarhole. This was Herbert Flagg's home; his grandfather Dennis had been a prominent spice and tea merchant in mid-1800s Boston. The house had a porch along its front, and a barn in back.

Flagg Home

Earlier owners were A. Flagg (1850s), P. Stone (1870), and storekeeper Ezra Comee, who sold it to Murray Flagg in 1898. Murray Flagg had been a member of the well-known Vigilance Committee of

San Francisco in the early 1850s. His grandson Herbert had been a realtor before retiring to Dana. When he sold out, he relocated to Pembroke. Donald Howe states that Herbert furnished his new home with many antiques purchased at auctions in the Swift River valley.

The dirt road to the right was the Tamplin Road. The open cellarhole located beween the left side of the Tamplin Road and the next road was Nellie Shattuck's home. It had the appearance of a small cottage, with an ell. There was a barn behind it. Her father, Irving T. Shattuck, had run a store in the village for many years before World War I. She was the last librarian for the village of Dana Common. Earlier owners of this home were J. Giddings (1857), F.Amsden (1870), and Larned Fisher (1900). Nellie Shattuck moved to Orange when she left Dana.

Nellie Shattuck's Home

If you continue up the Tamplin Road, there are two open cellarholes on the left, before crossing a brook. The first one was a home last owned by Rollin Doubleday. Earlier owners included John Johnson (middle 1800s) and Mrs. A. Guild (1898).

The second cellarhole was the Melzar Bates home after 1917. This was formerly I. T. Shattuck's home when he ran the store in the village; J.S. Brown owned it in the middle 1800s. It was a six room house, with a barn in the back. Bates was the last warden of the town poor farm, and also served the town as road superintendent.

There were two homes on this road after it crosses the brook. The first one, on the left, was the Lauriston Stone place, last owned by the Laura Stone estate (it was J. Moore's in 1870). This was a two story home, with a 1 1/2 story attached section. A pile of stones marks the house site. There was a barn just up the road.

Lauriston Stone Home

About 800 feet further up the road was the Charles Almquist farm. The house was on the left, and two barn cellarholes on the right. There are only a couple more cellarholes near the northern end of the Tamplin Road's three mile length up to Gates 38 and 39.

Back at the common, a paved road veers off to the northwest on the left side of the Shattuck cellarhole. This is identified by a sign installed in 1993 as the Skinner Hill Road. The filled-in cellarhole on the right (after you pass by the Shattuck barn site) was the home of Milton Vaughn after 1911. The barn site was a bit further up the road. This was the location of the last post office in the village. Mrs. Ethel White was the postmistress here when the office was closed on July 30, 1938. She and her husband removed to West Brookfield. Earlier owners of this included G. Bramman (1850s), S. W. Amsden (1870), and A. W. Doane (1898).

The last cellarhole on the right side of the

Milton Vaughn Home (Mrs. White, Dana's last Postmistress, is standing in front)

road before the brook was one of the buildings of N. L. Johnson's palm leaf hat shop from 1843-87. This was a cottage industry, with the palm leaf being imported by Johnson. The material was farmed out to local housewives, who would assemble the hats (or fans), then bring them to the shop. This was the original "piece work," the women being paid so much for each piece (hat or fan) completed. The shop would finish them off, then ship them out to wholesalers. In 1866, Sarah Lloyd, one of Johnson's workers, was lauded for earning $221.20 in 73 days of sewing shaker hoods on a machine.

The rest of the trip up Skinner Hill road beyond the brook is detailed in Chapter 17.

Back at the northwest side of Dana Common, there is a large cellarhole south of the Skinner Hill Road, on the western end of the common. This was the Eagle House or Hotel. The 2 1/2 story building had fifteen rooms. A porch ran along the side facing the common, and four pillars on the side facing West Main St. A stone wall along the left side of the Skinner Hill Road marks the site of the barn (and livery stable) serving the hotel.

A hotel was operated near this site as early as the 1830s, known as the Flagg Tavern. One Butterfield owned it afterwards. Joel Johnson bought and moved the 15 room building to its present site and rebuilt it in 1843. When the town voted to ban the sale of alcohol after the Civil War, Johnson closed the hotel rather than run it "dry." He ran a store in the building until his death in 1891.

Frank Grover, one of the Selectmen, bought the place in 1893. He reopened it as a hotel, renaming it the Eagle House. Grover added the piazza in 1894. He often hosted banquets for parties of sleighers and other travelers who came here. Frank Grover moved to North Dana in 1896, turning over the management of the hotel to his brother John, who ran it until his death. David Kennedy, who also ran the Mount L Hotel in North Dana for a time, succeeded Grover as owner. When Kennedy died in 1928, his heir James sold the property to the Water Commission. It was demolished in 1936.

Proceeding along West Main St. (the paved road), there is a cellarhole just west of the hotel one. This was a long plain building, with a barn sized doorway on the left, next to an attached shed. There was also a barn west of the shed. The doorway ramp now leads to an empty foundation. This building once housed N. L. Johnson's palm leaf factory, then I.T. Shattuck's store. The last owner of this property was Howard Cotton, who used it for storage.

Continuing down the street, on the right are the cellarholes of the barn, then the home of Ernest and Goldie Carrington. After selling out in 1931,

From Left:Carrington's,Cotton's barns,Eagle Hotel

they moved to Belchertown. Earlier owners of this place included Frank Johnson (1898), C.W. Pierce, Clara Belle Stone (1901-18), and Matthew Fraser (1918-21). This 2 1/2 story house had a two story porched ell attached, and sheds in back. In 1932, a Mr. Ice bought this for removal.

The paved road that continues straight down a hill past the Carrington's is the old road to Greenwich Village. This is covered in Chapter 18.

At the west end of Dana Common, opposite Carrington's, there is a road to the left. This once passed by Pottapaug Pond on its way to Greenwich Village. This road is described in a Chapter 19.

There is a filled-in cellarhole on the west side of this junction. This was the Etta Brown home after 1923. Earlier owners included S.F. Brown, one Lynch, Frank Stevens, and N.L. Johnson. There was a large barn attached to an ell along the left side of the house. The porch, which ran along the side of the house facing the road to Pottapaug Pond, had nicely fluted supporting posts.

Darling's (left) and Etta Brown's

We will now proceed back eastward along the south side of West Main St. The house on the east corner of the junction was owned by Samuel Darling from 1924. Earlier owners were C.Johnson in the middle 1800s, and Robert Marsh. This 2 1/2 story house had a small ell on the east side with an entrance, and a nice small covered doorway. There was a barn in the back of the lot.

The next house to the east was owned by Daniel Shea, a Springfield man. His widow Gertrude sold it to the Water Commission. It was a typical "I" style house, with a small ell on the west side, and a car garage in back. Mr. and Mrs. S. Lincoln owned this in the late 1800s.

Daniel Shea Home

The house to the east of Shea's was not only an interesting building, but the cellarhole holds a surprise for the visitor. This was Grace Dunn's home. Earlier owners included A. Ellis (1850s), Mrs. Stevens (1870), Martha Richardson (1898), and A. Johnson. A large 2 1/2 story dwelling, it had a porch around the front and east

Grace Dunn Home

side, and stretched back from the street to a small two-section barn. If one looks into the cellarhole today, there is an old safe lying there! A possible explanation for this could be that when Mrs. Dunn had to move out, she didn't want to pay to have the safe shipped. After being emptied, it was left behind when the house was demolished.

A bit east of the Dunn cellarhole is the site of a home and barn owned by S. D. Williams in the 1850s, then by A. Gorham in 1870. It was owned by A.W. Doane when it burned in September, 1894.

The next cellarhole is distinguished by its concrete foundation walls. This was one of the most important buildings on the common; the village store and long-time post office. This was a long, 2 1/2 story building, with a shed attached to the left rear. A porch along the front was partly built over on the left side to provide an enclosed entrance to the store. In its last years, there was a single gasoline pump in front.

There was a store on this site before the Civil War; N. L. Johnson (see next cellarhole) operated it for a time in the 1840s and 1850s. Other proprietors included James B. Brown, Arthur Whipple, S.H. Hellyar, Frank Stevens, and Howard Cotton (1917-1935). Many of the store operators also served as the village postmaster. In Cotton's time, there was an apartment in the rest of the building. This building was demolished in 1936.

Dana Common Store

The house located east of the store was a three-story, mansard-roofed building that could have been called a mansion. This was the home of the Johnsons, one of the wealthiest families in Dana's history. The house had a large covered doorway in front; there was a barn next to the store. N.L. Johnson completely remodeled this in 1884, adding the mansard roof, bay windows, and piazzas. Most of the cellarholes of both house and barn are still visible.

Johnson Home

Nathaniel L. Johnson (1822-1902) ran the village store, was postmaster, and a manufacturer of palm leaf hats. He served the town in many official capacities, and was the only resident to serve as a State Senator. He spoke at the town's centennial in 1901. His son John (1865-1929), became a prominent lawyer in Worcester, but returned to live out his life in Dana. John John-

Nathaniel L. Johnson

son was,like his father, active in civic affairs. John's daughter, Marion, lived into her mid-nineties. She recalled witnessing the Dana centennial in 1901 when attending a comemorative event on the common in 1988. Marion, and Frank Johnson (a relative) sold the home to the Water Commission.

Just east of the Johnson cellarhole, a narrow roadway separates it from a stone wall. This driveway led to the Cooley and Langley homes. On the left side of this roadway is a wonderful pebbled-stone wall. Parts of it extend around the back of a cellarhole, which was the Edgar Vaughn home. This 1 1/2 story dwelling had several large trees in front of it; some of these are still standing. The Vaughns settled here in 1899; J. S. Brown had been an earlier owner. This 8 room home burned in April, 1937.

O.E. Vaughn Home (Note wall at lower right)

Myron Vaughn recalled that, as a boy, he helped his father cement the stones together to build the wall. They got some of the stones from local streambeds. This wall, in remarkably good condition, is one of the highlights of the Common. Many people have photographed or painted scenes of this wall.

The cellarhole behind the Vaughn one on the left side of the roadway was the six room Roger Langley home. Langley, a teacher at the Eagle Brook School in Deerfield, bought this in 1926 from Eugene Sweetland. Earlier owners included Larned

Fisher (1870) and Hannah Doubleday (1898). The Dwight Cooley home stood next to the tree at the end of the roadway on the right. An earlier owner was J. W. Brown. The cellarhole of the barn is partly visible on the right, behind the Johnson cellarhole. Dwight Cooley moved to Petersham; Les Cooley was one of the last people to leave the Common.

Dwight Cooley Home

The field behind the Cooley homesite was reclaimed in the late 1980s by the M.D.C. If you walk to the far end of it, you can see an arm of the reservoir.

The next cellarhole on the main street, east of the Vaughn one was the Congregational Church edifice. Such churches can be found on town commons all over New England. They are in almost every Massachusetts town because Congregationalism was the officially recognized religion in the state until 1830. Ironically, the first regular Congregational parish in Dana was located in the hamlet of Storrsville (See Chapter 20).

The "Orthodox Congregational Church of Dana Centre" was organized in 1852. J. S. Brown and his wife deeded the lot for the building to the society for $50.00. The church was erected the following year, and Rev. John Keep was transferred from the Storrsville parish to this one. He delivered the dedication sermon on November 15, 1853, and remained here until 1861.

Other long-serving pastors included Rev. Harlan Paige (1893-1912 - who also served Hardwick), and Rev. Henry M. Brown (1921-37 - who also served the North Dana Methodists - see under his home in Chapter 17).

Marcille Home and Dana Congregational Church

During part of the church's existence, it had a domed steeple. This was replaced with a pointed wooden spire in 1928. Horse sheds in the back collapsed after a heavy snowfall in the winter of 1920. A fire broke out in the church during a service late in 1924, but it was put out by the parishoners. The last service held here was on July 31, 1938, with 60 people present.

After selling out to the Water Commission, the church donated the sum of $10,700 to the Mass. Congregational Society. The bell that once hung in the church's belfrey is now at the Hope Congregational Church in Worcester, MA. The front walk to the church is still evident, as is most of the cellarhole.

The last cellarhole on our tour, east of the Congregational Church, was that of the smallest house on the common. An old dwelling, it was last owned by Josephine Marcille. She and her blacksmith husband had bought it from Lula Price Spooner in 1904. A Mrs. Smith, and later. A.W. Doane had lived there before. If you walk around to the back, you can see there was an elaborate cellar. A three room addition was built onto the back of the four room home shortly after the Marcilles moved in. There was also a shed in the back.

This was the second Dana home of the tragic blacksmith, Moses Marcille. His first home and smithy in Dana, located a few hundred feet to the east, was mentioned in the last chapter. After that home burned in a fire, the Marcilles lived in Fall River for five years. Then Marcille moved back to Dana, resuming his blacksmithing at this location

On March 21, 1907, after an argument, Marcille shot his wife twice, then pointed the gun at his head and "blew out his brains." as a contemporary account put it. Despite her wounds, the wife survived, living in the house for another two decades, until it was sold to the Water Commission. (For more on this, see Chapter 40 in the author's 1993 book *"Strange Tales From Old Quabbin"*)

Before concluding the tour of Dana, some features of the common itself should be mentioned. From 1892, the common was surrounded by a low two-rail white fence. While none of that fence is still in existence, some of the Y-shaped posts which once supported the railing along the road in front of the town hall can still be found. At least one of the trees still standing on the common dates from an Arbor Day planting in 1892.

Dana celebrated its centennial as an incorporated town with a big celebration on the common on August 22, 1901. Ex-Senator N. L. Johnson delivered the Historical address. All of the buildings facing the common were decorated with bunting, and there were tents erected on the common itself. A large crowd enjoyed the festivities. A more subdued program was held to celebrate the 125th anniversary of the town in 1926, as everyone correctly presumed this would be the town's last great gathering.

There were three monuments on the common during the last years of the town. One was a cannon, probably a souvenir of the Civil War, located near the center of the green. The base foundation stone for this gun, which pointed eastward, can still be seen. A walkway that ran past the cannon from opposite the Flagg House toward the store can also be seen.

Dana War Memorial and Cannon

Another monument was a stone marker honoring the town's war veterans; this was located near the west side of the green. A bronze plate set into it listed all of the town's veterans through the First World War. It was dedicated on Memorial Day, 1924. A flagpole stood behind this spot for many years before the monument was erected.

The last monument on the common was the Hosea Ballou memorial. Located east of the cannon, this was another bronze plaque set into a conical stone. This monument was erected by the Dana Women's Club in 1923. It commemorates the fact that Ballou, a pioneer Unitarian Universalist minister, lived in the southeast part of town from about 1794 to 1803.

Ballou Monument

Ballou (1771-1852) was a native of Richmond, NH, where a marker noting his birthplace can be seen on Route 32. He wrote books, sermons, and hymns promoting his faith, and founded a periodical, the *Universalist Expositor*. Ballou spent his last 35 years in Boston, although he preached around the nation.

Hosea Ballou

The cannon and these two monuments were moved to the Quabbin Park Cemetery in Ware, where they can be seen near the entrance (See Chapter 5).

A cistern was located on the southwest side of the common for many years, across the street from the store. It was a large metal cylinder. This cistern, and all but three of the buildings on the common were served by a private well located north of the school.

Until the early 1990s, people hiking or bicycling to Dana Common had no proper way to "answer the call of nature." Recently, a portable toilet has been placed at the Dwight Cooley cellarhole during the summer months. This is in conjunction with the placing of other toilets at a few shoreline points for the convenience of fishermen.

There have been some proposals over the years to erect small markers to identify the cellarholes on Dana Common, or even to picture the buildings. So far, this has not come to pass, perhaps because the reservation managers feel that this would only encourage more visits to the area. Some sort of marking system, even using numbered stakes, would be better than nothing, and would not detract from the natural beauty of the site.

It should be remembered that even though the Dana area seems to be quite "natural" (other than the roads and stone walls), it was inhabited by white families for a century and a half, and perhaps by Native Americans in earlier times.

MAP OF DANA COMMON

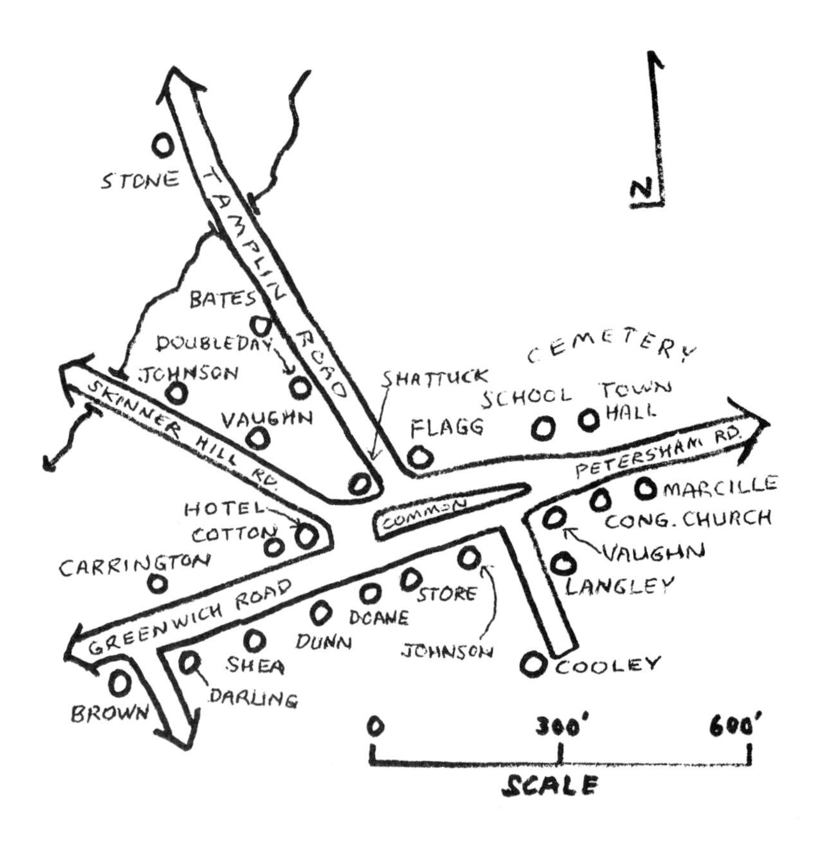

Chapter 17 - SKINNER HILL ROAD

In the Dana Common chapter, the first couple of sites on the paved Skinner Hill Road were noted. In this chapter, the rest of the 1 1/2 mile road will be described. This road goes up a long, steep hill much of the way.

Not far after crossing the brook, (where the road is dirt) and starting up the hill, there are cellarholes on both sides of the road, at breaks in the stone walls. The one on the right was the Brown home; the barn was on the left. This 1 1/2 story dormered cape, with an ell to the left, was known as "The Locusts."

This was the farm of Timothy Stone until his death in 1892. His daughter, Mrs. Elizabeth Bedell, was a teacher at Dana Center school during the Civil War. She was later a businesswoman in New York. One of her daughters married E. F. Bristol; the other, Adele, married Rev. Henry M. Brown of New York. Mrs. Bedell spent her last dozen years at this home, with Mr. and Mrs. Brown, until her death at age 94 in 1933.

"The Locusts"

Rev. Henry M. Brown was the last minister of the Dana Congregational and North Dana Methodist parishes. Brown and his family had summered here many years before he accepted the dual ministry in 1921. He was the only valley resident listed in *"Who's Who in America"* in the late 1920s.

Not far beyond Brown's, the road crosses over

a brook, then there is an attractive cellarhole on the right, with some large hydrangea bushes growing in front of it. This was the summer home of Cambridge resident Louis Wells. He was a teacher at a Boston industrial school. After selling out, they bought a home in West Orange.

Wells Residence

Earlier owners included T. Stevens in the mid-1800s, then F.F. Simonds. This two story home had a pillared porch, a broad dormered window (built in 1925) and a long extension to the right. The cellarhole includes a pebbled front wall, and a root cellar, making it worth exploring.

A dirt road goes off to the right past the Wells cellarhole; a recent sign identifies it as the Whitney Hill Road. It runs northward three miles through what was a mainly uninhabited section toward Gates 39 and 38. About two miles up this road on the left was the Stone Cemetery, which contained 41 graves.

About a quarter of a mile north of the Wells place on the Whitney Hill Road are the Augusta Tolman barn and house cellarholes on the left. Earlier owners included Stephen King, then Ezra Greenleaf. This 2 1/2 story farmhouse had a porch facing south; there was a barn off to the left. A walled-in area (and old stock pen?) is across the road on the right.

Back at the road junction, on the northwest corner is the partly filled-in cellarhole of the

Elias F. Bristol home; the barn was across the road. This was a 1 1/2 story cape, with 9 rooms, and an extension to the right. An earlier owner was F. Paine. Bristol was a selectmen in town for many years. One of his sons, Kenneth, sent snapshots of many homes in Dana to friends as greeting cards. Some of the Bristols moved to Athol after selling out.

E. F. Bristol Home

The Skinner Hill road, now paved, continues uphill, passing two sets of farm sites on both sides of the road. In both cases, the house was on the right, and the barns on the left side of the road. The first one was the Jeremiah Lynch place (Stone's in 1870, Russell's in 1898). The porch of this 1 1/2 story place was remodeled in the 1920s; the cellarhole was obliterated. Part of the barn foundation across the road is still visible. The Lynches ran a poultry farm here; chicken houses were in back of the main house.

The next place was the home of storekeeper Howard Cotton, who came here during World War I. This place was previously owned by the Tolman family for many years. Part of the house cellarhole is discernable; there were sheds and a camp near it. The foundation walls of the two barns are visible across the road. Cotton removed to North Brookfield after selling out.

There is an old wood road off that drops steeply off to the left after Cotton's cellarholes.

It leads to the paved road running west from West Main St. out of Dana. There is an old cellarhole on the right not very far in.

After rounding a corner, there is a section of the Skinner Hill Road lined with dug out spots on the right. This was a gravel pit used by the town. The next cellarhole on this road was about 3/4 of a mile up the road, at the top of the stonewall-lined hill. This was the long, 1 1/2 story home of Horatio Eddy after 1905. All of the cellarholes here were obliterated, although a few bricks from the house can be found to the left of a low banking on the right side of the road. Two barns were east of the house. Two parallel stone walls run behind the house site.

There was an apple orchard here; the fields were recently reclaimed from the pines planted when the reservoir was built. The Amsden family owned this home in the mid-1800s; later it was owned by R. C. and Alice Beecher. Eddy moved to Taunton after selling out for much less than his asking price of $15,840.00.

220 feet west of the Eddy place, on the opposite side of the road, is the Dana town hearse house lot. There is no cellarhole at this site, which is at a break in the stone wall along the road. In the 1800s, when there were few funeral directors, many New England towns bought a hearse for public convenience. This site was chosen because it was halfway between the two villages. It

Dana Hearse House *(MDC Photo)*

was deeded to the town in 1878 by Emily Amsden. Just west of this spot is an enclosure made up of tall stone walls. This might have been an animal pen or pound.

Beyond this point, the road decends steeply around a sharp corner. This was named Deadman's Curve, beacuse there was at least one fatal auto accident here. The dirt road to the left leads down to a crossroads near the shoreline.

The cellarhole on the northwest side of this shoreline crossroads was that of Joseph W. Stevens. This two story house ran westerly, with an ell and shed back toward the barn. Members of the Stevens family had owned this for several decades when it burned on December 20, 1928. Joseph moved to Doubleday Village after the fire; he died there in December, 1932, at the age of 73.

The road on the south side of the Stevens crossroads goes southward about a mile, passing the Tetzlaff and Towne cellarholes before it comes to the shoreline.

Back at the Skinner Hill Road, about 400 feet beyond the junction with the dirt road, are breaks in the stone walls. Two sides of the foundation of a barn are on the left. The house cellarhole, after a brook, was obliterated. This was the Skinner farm for many years.

Benjamin Skinner, a Revolutionary War veteran, settled here shortly after Dana became a town. His grandson Sardius ran this farm during the

Skinner Home *(MDC Photo)*

late 1800s. Estelle Whitaker Skinner sold this property to the Water Commission, then moved to Tully, where she died at the age of 75 in 1936. Bert Aber (of Needham) rented this from the Commission for two years, raising chickens until he died there in November, 1936.

Not far after the Skinner place, the paved road reaches the shoreline. Look for a stone marker on the right where the road meets the high water mark. This honors the state game warden after whom this was named Graves Landing.

MAP OF SKINNER HILL, GREENWICH, POTTAPAUG POND RDS.

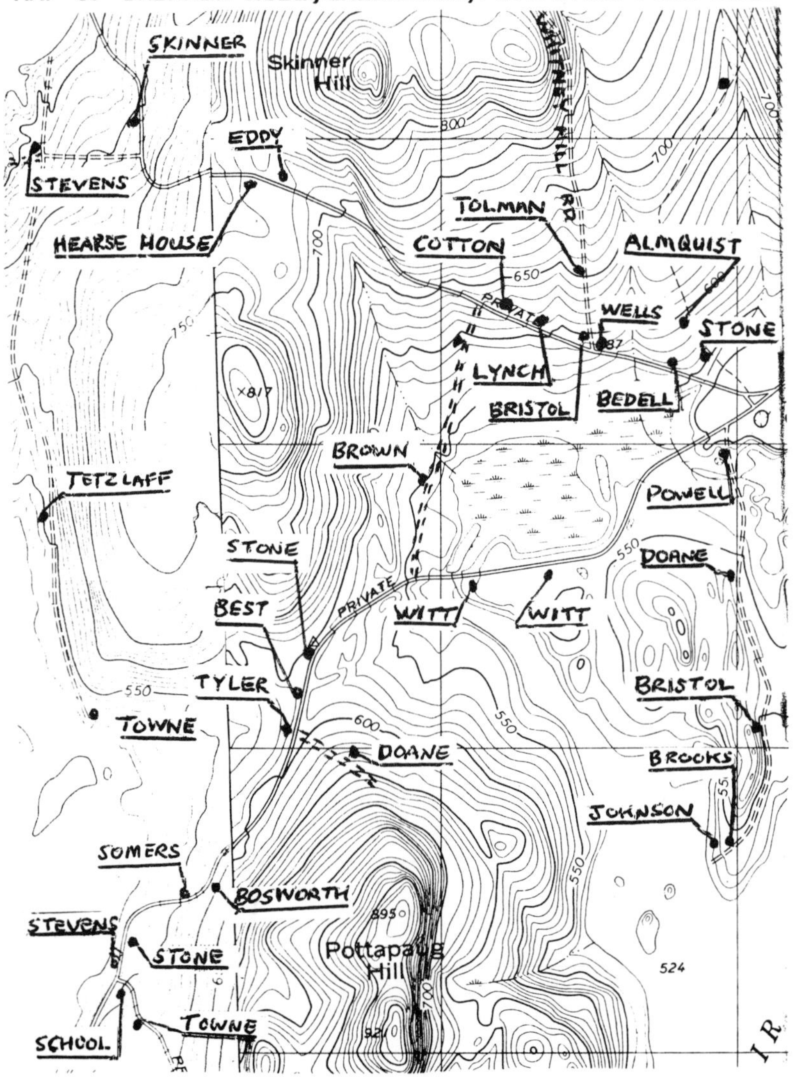

Chapter 18 GREENWICH ROAD (DANA)

This chapter will describe the paved road running west from the junction on the west side of Dana Common. This road goes by two large swamps, and skirts the north side of Pottapaug Hill before going into the water two miles from the Common. There are some fine vistas along this road.

The first house site on this road past the junction with the Pottapaug Pond Road was a small cottage, on the left; the foundation of this was obliterated. Etta Brown was the owner of this; she also owned the house back on the corner. The road then goes down a short hill to a flat section, with swampy land on both sides.

About a half mile west of Dana Common, there are two cellarholes on the left. Both of these were owned by members of the Witt family in the late 1800s. The first one is open, about 30 feet from the road, in a grove of pines. This place burned in the late 1800s.

The other Witt place was located on a slope just before the culvert over the second swamp on this road. The cellarhole of this long, 1 1/2 story place was obliterated. Owners of this included Albert and Hattie Witt, Almira Tyler, then Levrett Best, who sold it to Redford Johnson in 1919. Johnson called it "Best Farm."

Shortly past the swamp, as the road heads up a hill, there is an old stone wall - lined road on the right. This passes by the old cellarholes of a farm owned by Sullivan Brown in the late 1800s. The open L-shaped cellarhole of the house is on a knoll on the left. On a hillside behind this, the lonely grave of a child has stood for decades. There is another cellarhole on the left before this lane joins the Skinner Hill Road.

The paved road continues up along the north edge of Pottapaug Hill. There are two home sites on the right. The first site is obliterated. It was the home of Walter and Warren Stone in 1900. The second site belonged to J. Lincoln in 1870, and Levrett Best around 1900. Ulysses Towne was the last owner of this L-shaped 5 room home. The cellarhole is filled in; part of the back wall of the barn foundation is still visible.

Shortly after these sites (which are in an area recently cleared of timber), there is a grassed-over dirt road on the left. This leads to the cellarhole of the Albert Doane place, known as Pottapaug Farm. This had been owned by several members of the Doane family before it burned in the early 1900s. There are large stone walls here.

A short distance north of this farm site, there is a large hole in the ground. That, and bits and pieces of wreckage mark the crash site of a small military plane here in the 1950s. If you search the woods southeast of the farm site, along the side of Pottapaug Hill, you may find "Indian Kitchen," a rock formation that some say was a campsite used by the native Indians.

Returning to the paved road, the next house site is on the right, in a cut in the banking just past the old grassy road. This was Emond's in 1857, Peckham's in 1870; Lewis Merritt and Henry Tyler lived there in the 1890s.

The next site is before the road goes downhill at a corner. The Loren Bosworth farm is on both sides of the road. There are many large stone walls here. The cellarholes here are obliterated; the barn was on the right, and the 12 room house and a barn were on the left. George Durkee lived here from 1909-19.

A house site is on the right just past Bosworth's; the cellarhole was obliterated. Margaret King sold this to Hannah Somers in 1925. These last two properties were owned by L. Hale in 1857, L. Sears in 1870, Joseph Lincoln in the 1880s, and the Tylers around 1900.

After rounding another corner, the shoreline of the reservoir is visible through the trees on the right. There is a barn cellarhole here; this was part of the Oscar Stone place. The filled-in cellarhole of the 1 1/2 story cape is on the left, behind a stone wall. I. Town(e) owned this in 1857; the Horr family in the late 1800s.

There is a road to the right, which went to North Dana. It goes into the water after only a few feet. The filled-in cellarhole of the Henry Stevens place is just after this on the right. This was J. Parkhurst's in 1857, and J. White's in 1870. J. W. Russell, in his 1986 book, states that this building was moved to the Bement School grounds at Old Deerfield.

The Greenwich Road goes straight down a slope into the water past here. A small district school was located on the left side of the road, just after a dirt road. The cellarhole was filled in. This was discontinued by the town around 1912, and sold to Ulysses Towne.

Old West School *(MDC Photo)*

The dirt road off to the left was called the Southworth Road in 1900. After a curve, there are several cellarholes on both sides of the road. This was the Oscar Towne farm, which had been previously owned by several generations of the Doubleday family. The cellarhole of the 1 1/2 story house (with an ell) on the right was obliterated. The barn cellarholes on both sides of the road are filled in. Ulysses Towne was the last owner.

The Southworth Road goes for a mile around the south side of Pottapaug Hill. After passing a dead end road to the right, it comes out at Fishing Area #3. Since it is over a mile hike out to Gate 43 from the there, one can see that only an ambitious hiker would try to make a loop hike to Gate 40 (via. Hardwick Center and Route 32A) with this route!

Chapter 19 POTTAPAUG POND ROAD

The road to Pottapaug Pond is off West Main St. at Dana Common, It was known as the Thayer Road in 1898. Most of it is still paved.

The road begins by decending into a small hollow. A filled-in cellarhole on the right here was the Gertrude Powell home (J. F. Johnson's in 1898). It was a two story peak-roofed place, dating from the late 1800s, with a shed in back. At one time, it was called "Polly's Pocket Book." Mrs. Powell's husband, Dr. Lyman Powell, was a professor and an Episcopal rector in New Jersey. Their son, Talcott, was a journalist. The family of Ray Wildes lived here in the 1930s; they later moved to Petersham.

Powell Residence

An arm of the reservoir is visible from the Powell cellarhole. The M.D.C. has planted flowering shrubs across the road. Before the Civil War, a boot shop was located on the west side of the road where a brook runs under it.

The road continues almost a mile down to the former Pottapaug Pond. The old G. W. Doane place was about a quarter of a mile down this road, after a short climb. The cellarhole of this 12 room, L-shaped 2 1/2 story home was filled in. The front steps are still visible behind a front wall on the right. The last owner was Victoria Doane, who moved to Orange.

Further along the road, there is a cleared area on the right. Stone walls line the hillside here. On the northern side of the north wall is the site of Ashley Bristol's camp, which was on his father's property. There is no cellarhole. This 1 1/2 story camp had a lattice-work porch base.

Ashley Bristol's Camp

The road continues past some ledges on the left, then gradually goes down to the water, just above the old bed of Pottapaug Pond. This pond was fed and drained by the East Branch of the Swift River. so it was inundated by the reservoir. Several homes and camps dotted its shores. A couple of cellarholes are visible on the right side of the road just before it goes under the water.

The first cellarhole (partly filled-in) is near the corner of two stone walls beside the road. The was the old Brooks farm. The other one is on a ledge, close to the shore. There are stones and bricks from the chimney here. A driveway to the road is still discernable. This was Dr. Rexford K. Johnson's summer home, "Camp Gilead."

Rexford K. Johnson was the Chairman of the Board of the Alexander Hamilton Institute in New York, which had been founded by his father Joseph F. Johnson. The latter's father had run the store in Storrsville for a time.

Johnson owned much of the land in this section. He told Walter Clark that one of the back lots was called "White Horse Pasture," as his fa-

"Camp Gilead"

ther had traded a white horse to obtain it.

Two famous people lived briefly in the Pottapaug Pond area. In both cases, the exact location is difficult to determine. Hosea Ballou, the pioneer Unitarian minister, lived in this part of town at the time it was incorporated (See Chapter 16).

General Leonard Wood was Theodore Roosevelt's commanding officer in the Spanish-American War, and a leading contender for the 1920 Republican Presidential nomination, He lived here for a few years during his boyhood in the 1860s, when his father was a local doctor.

Chapter 20 STORRSVILLE (GATE 41)

Storrsville was a hamlet at a crossroads near Rand Brook, in the southeastern part of Dana. In the second quarter of the 1800s, it was a thriving village, with several families, a pocketbook factory, church, school, hotel, store, smithy, and a debating society.

The village was called Tinkertown when it was part of Petersham. Its later name honors Rev. Emory Storrs, a Congregational minister from New Braintree. He established a mission church here in 1832, in a building on the northwest corner of the crossroads. The first settled minister was Rev. Amos A. Dewey, who was buried in the cemetery just north of here after his death at the age of 36 in 1840. The last minister was Rev. John Keep, who moved with the parish to Dana Common in 1852.

Rev. John Keep
(From Keep Genealogy)

Originally part of Hardwick and Petersham, Storrsville was set off to Dana in 1842. Unfortunately, the village had just reached its peak. The pocketbook factory burned later that year, and the church parish was moved to Dana Common in 1853. The church building was moved to Brookfield, where it burned. The old hotel building burned in 1872.

A cheese factory operated for a short time on the southwest corner of the crossroads after the Civil War. In the same era, a saw and shingle mill was run with power from a millpond just upstream from the village. Part of the mill dam is visible on property last owned by Seth Carter.

In 1900, all that remained of "The Deserted Village" was the sawmill, two cemeteries, and a few houses; even the school had been closed. By the time the Water Commission began to buy up property in the valley, most of the land in this village was owned by three families; the Finns, Lindseys, and Marvells.

John and Josephine Finn owned the property north of the crossroads. The open cellarhole at the northwest corner there was the site of the church. then the Pollard home in 1870.

200 feet north of the crossroads was the cellarhole of the Finn's two-section house on the west side of the road; it is partly filled-in. A small cellarhole (a root cellar, or part of the barn) is on the east side of the road. This place had been owned by the William Smith family in the middle to late 1800s. The Finns moved to Rutland after selling their property.

About 250 feet behind the Finn house cellarhole is the partially walled-in site of the Richardson Cemetery. There were only 15 graves in this half-acre burial ground; all were moved out.

Bertha Lindsey owned the southwest corner of the junction, and most of the land on the southeast corner. Her husband Charles had been a carpenter and a school bus driver. The partly filled-in cellarhole on the southwest corner of the

Bertha Lindsey Home

crossroads was the cheese factory in 1870.

The open cellarhole of Bertha Lindsey's house is visible on the southeast side of the crossroads; it was 1 1/2 stories, with a porch, and had sheds in back. This had been owned by the Smith family in the late 1800s. The Lindsey's moved to Orange after selling out.

George Lindsey owned the 2 1/2 story house that was about 500 feet east of the crossroads, on the south side of the Barre-Dana road. This home, which had a porch, was owned by the Flaherty family in the late 1800s; Frank Dushon lived here in 1912. The back part of the cellarhole is still standing in a banking.

Across the road, just up from George Lindsey's, was the tenth-acre Hopkins Cemetery. There were 36 graves here before the Water Commission removed them. Stone walls enclose most of the site.

Guy Marvell owned almost 100 acres on the west side of the junction of Route 32A and the Barre-Dana Rd. Marvell and his mother Cora moved here from Prescott after his father died. She died here in 1938. He was one of the last landowners in the Swift River valley to settle with the Commission.

If you park at Gate 41, on the west side of Route 32A at the crossroads, Marvell's buildings are the impressive foundations and cellarholes on both sides of the road inside of the gate. His 2 1/2 story, ten room home is the first (open) cellarhole on the right; it was owned by the Grover family in the late 1800s. A cement structure is on one side of the foundation of the attached shed. The large barn cellarhole is just past this; another large cement structure is on one corner of this.

Seth Carter had owned the buildings on the left side of the road around 1900. Foundation walls of these can be seen.

There is a pond on the left after Marvell's cellarholes; this is just downstream from a small pond where Marvell ran a fish hatchery in the 1930s. The Water Commission knocked out Marvell's dam. He also raised poultry in several chicken houses here.

When his property was first appraised, Marvell

Marvell Home

asked $40,000 for it; he ended up with a little more than a quarter of that sum. A special legislative resolve was passed in 1945 to pay Marvell $4,160.16 to compensate him for loss of business due to the taking of his property. Moving out in 1944, he settled at the old Stone place just east of the village site, where he spent his last 25 years. Ernest Geoffrey of Hardwick paid the Water Commission $175.00 to remove the buildings on Marvell's former property.

This paved road goes into the water about a quarter mile in from Gate 41. This flowage is the northeasternmost part of the reservoir. Paths to the left and right along the shoreline are often used by shore fishermen.

MAP OF STORRSVILLE

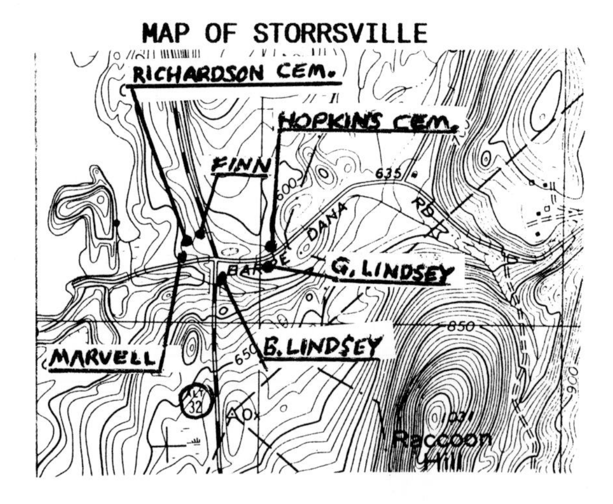

Chapter 21 THE PHANTOM RAILROAD

The Swift River valley was on the route of two railroads that were chartered in 1869. These were the Athol & Enfield RR, and the Massachusetts Central RR. The first line was completed through the valley in 1871 (see Chapter 12).

The second line began to build a railbed in Enfield, Greenwich, and Hardwick in 1871. The financial panic of 1873 prevented the corporation from completing the project. When the railroad was finally completed in 1887, the route was changed to run it through Ware and Bondsville, south of the original location. While this caused some in Hardwick to bemoan the "wasted efforts" done in the Swift River valley, nothing was ever done with the uncompleted railroad bed.

The remains of these efforts are quite evident in the western part of Hardwick, both within and outside of the Quabbin Reservation. To find these old cuts and fills, park at the lot outside of Gate 43 and 43A on the Greenwich Road in Hardwick. Walk along the road a few hundred feet to the west. If you look closely, you can see a sunken area on either side of the road at a curve. On the left, or south side of the road, a narrow path leads (over private property) to the bed from a point a few dozen feet east of the ravine. The path comes to the bed at a point where a dirt road makes a hairpin turn to join it. The railbed forms a straight, tree-lined pathway above most of the surrounding land for almost a half mile. There are two ponds cut in half by the bed, which add to the fine view from it.

On either side of the bed, where it runs along land nearly level with it, places can be discerned where dirt was dug out of the ground with shovels, and loaded onto horsedrawn carts. It was hauled to where it was dumped from the cart onto the end of the grade for fill. Some of the large rocks that were left behind can be seen. The workmen were paid around $1.75 - $2.00 per day for what must have been heavy labor.

At the end of this straight stretch, there is a short break in the bed for a dirt road to cross it. Just past this, the bed becomes a bit grown in; there is a bypass path to the left. Where the bypass rejoins the original bed, the causeway is at its highest to cross over Muddy Brook. There is a dip in the bed over a stone culvert, where the filling wasn't raised up to the level of the rest of the bed. The culvert, made up of stone slabs, is still in fairly good shape in spite of a century and a quarter of neglect.

Now on land of the New England Forestry Foundation, the bed is joined on the left by a dirt road, heading to a rough trail off to the right. A narrow stone culvert allows passage of a brook through the bed shortly after this; unless there is a tree trunk laying there, you may have to jump across it. After this, the bed is quite grown in, and muddy much of the year, as the ground around it is higher. In a few hundred more feet, the bed comes to an abrupt end in the woods, probably marking the boundary of a contractor's assigned section.

Inside of the Quabbin Reservation, the cuts and fills of the bed are somewhat spottier. An impressive, but overgrown section of fill runs southeast from the junction of the roads from Gates 43A and 44. The continuation of the bed is a bit difficult to spot west of here; one has to look for the cuts of the bed in the woods to the left near a dirt road that runs northwest of the aforementioned junction. After a deep, unfinished cut, the fill is visible from the north side of

A Section of the RR Bed ***(M. Watt)***

the paved access road to Shaft 12 above the terrain of the downsloping hillside.

The bed can be followed without too much difficulty from here westward, in spite of a few breaks. It crosses the dirt Fitzpatrick Road that runs down from the access road into the reservoir. Just below this crossing, there are several well-preserved cellarholes at a road junction near the shoreline. The ones to the left of the junction were the old Walker family farm. It was a 2 1/2 story home, with a barn and several sheds nearby.

This was the birthplace of William H. Walker, author of "EZ," and his brother George. Both were prominent businessmen in Greenwich for many years. George returned to live here in 1906. Walter Clark called George one of "the two largest breeders of turkeys in the valley."

George Walker Home

The other cellarholes here, just north of the road junction, were the Hall farm for many decades. There was a 1 1/2 story home, with a large barn east of it, next to the current shoreline. Alfred Hall sold this to the Commission.

The railroad bed has another large gap as it approaches the shoreline east of the South Baffle Dam. Just east from where it goes into the reservoir, there is a very steep cut. At the shore of the reservoir, the bed forms a small peninsula that juts out into the Quabbin. When the water is low, this peninsula is quite noticeable from either a fishing boat, or from the South Baffle Dam, looking east.

To learn more about the story of this "Phantom Railroad," read Chapter One of the author's 1993 book *"Strange Tales From Old Quabbin."*

Chapter 22 THE GOLF COURSE CLUBHOUSE

One of the best preserved buildings in the valley was left standing on its original site. This is the clubhouse built for the Dugmar Golf Course in Greenwich. This roofless stone structure, with its massive front steps, is visible on the southeast shore of Curtis Hill Island.

Golf Course Clubhouse

The golf course was the brainchild of two executives of the Chapman Valve Co. of Springfield; John J. Duggan (Secretary-Treasurer), and Thomas Maher (President). Beginning in 1924, they purchased a 100+ acre farm in Greenwich and two adjoining parcels for less than $10,000. These were located between Curtis Hill and Curtis Pond.

The stone clubhouse was erected in 1926; then a nine-hole golf course laid out by noted designer Orrin Smith in 1928. Duggan and Maher named this "great plaything and hobby of theirs" by combining their last names.

The two executives and their friends often rode up the "rabbit line" (Athol Branch of the B & A RR) to enjoy their resort on weekends or summer vactions. A few local boys made some money caddying or doing other work for these "big shots." Even though prohibition (of alcoholic beverages) was in effect during the first few years of the course's existence, it was said that booze flowed rather freely at the club.

In any event, this, like all properties within the projected reservoir area, was slated for purchase by the Water Commission. The owners of the course incresed their selling price from $200,000 to $436,500, which was refused. This resulted in several referee hearings and court cases, which dragged on until 1937. The final verdict was that they received (including interest) $179,042; a return of over four times their original investment!

When the destruction of buildings was taking place in the valley in the late 1930s, the original farmstead, outbuildings, and clubhouse roof on the property were taken down. The walls of the stone clubhouse building were left standing, probably due to the fact that they were to end up above the waterline, on an island.

Today, one can ride right past this ghostly shell of a building in a fishing boat, although it is illegal to land on the island to walk up into it. Landlubbers can get a view of the building from Shaft 12, on the southeastern shore of the reservoir.

The Shaft 12 building houses the intake for the aqueduct running eastward to Wachusett Reservoir. It can be reached by walking two miles down the paved access road running west from the junction of the roads from Gates 44 and 43A. When you reach the intake building, stay on the north side of it, and scan the islands to the northwest with a pair of field glasses for a view of the impressive stone ruin.

Chapter 23 SITES OUTSIDE OF THE QUABBIN

This chapter notes the museum of the Swift River Valley Historical Society, and three public buildings that were moved from the valley. All but one of these is open for public visiting.

Swift River Valley Historical Society (SRVHS) Museum Complex

This organization was founded in 1935, to propagate the memory of the four lost towns and New Salem. It had no permanent home for three decades, but held annual meetings in the New Salem area.

In the early 1960s, negotiations were held with the M.D.C. to allow the SRVHS to obtain a house on Elm St., in North New Salem. This 1816 house was owned by the Whittaker family in its early years, then was in the Clary family off and on from the 1880s until it was purchased by the Water Commission in the late 1930s. Harriet Clary was the last owner.

Robert Bullard rented it from Commission after he moved out of his home at the site of the former Herrick's Tavern. The house was named the Whittaker-Clary House by the SRVHS when they purchased it. This building has served as the society's main building ever since.

The Prescott Historical Society was founded in 1932. In 1949, it purchased the 1836 North Prescott Methodist-Episcopal Church that stood outside of Gate 20. The building was moved to a lot across the street from the entrance to Mahar High School in Orange, where it stood as the society's meeting place and museum.

When the Prescott Historical Society disbanded in 1985, it turned the building over to the SRVHS, who moved it onto their grounds. The main church hall serves as a meeting room for society functions, and a museum of Prescott materials. The basement houses the society's office and archives (including genealogy materials).

Behind the house stands a large red barn; this was used for many years for the storage of large objects, including the old Dana fire truck.

In the late 1980s, a generous member of the society donated funds for a new wooden storage building, which was erected behind the church.

The main house is still used for the display of most of the society's artifacts. There are separate rooms for Dana, Enfield, Greenwich, and New Salem, as well as an art room, and a schoolroom.

The museum is open on Wednesday and Sunday afternoons from 2-4 PM in July and August, and Sundays through September. Annual meetings are held on the third Saturday of June and September. There is an admission charge, which is not much lower than the annual membership fee. The latter includes a newsletter subscription.

OTHER BUILDINGS

Several dozen buildings were removed from the Swift River valley before it was inundated. Most of these were traced by J. W. Russell in his 1986 publication "Buildings and Bells," (which was out of print in 1994). The three prominent public buildings to survive in their original form (all from Prescott) are detailed here.

The Prescott Congregational Church

This building originally stood at the crossroads known as Prescott Hill village, in the southern part of that town. It was erected in 1848, replacing an earlier edifice. The structure was raised up a few feet in the early 1900s.

In 1924, the parish deeded its property to the Mass. Congregational Missionary Society, who sold it to the Water Commission in 1928. They received $16,000 for it. The last service was held here by Rev. Caleb Smith on July 1, 1928.

In 1930, Joseph Skinner, the Holyoke silk manufacturer, bought this building and moved it to South Hadley. It is now located on Rte. 116, just north of Mt. Holyoke College. A spire was added to the rebuilt church, and many items of historical interest are displayed in it. Now a museum, it is open to the public from 2-5 PM on Wednesdays and Sundays, May through October.

Prescott Congregational Church

Atkinson Hollow Tavern

This building was erected in 1795, in the section of South New Salem that later became part of the Prescott hamlet of Atkinson Hollow. Revolutionary War veteran John Atkinson built this as a home, but opened a tavern here shortly after the town was incorporated in 1822.

Cheney and Fred Abbott lived here in the middle 1800s, then Dr. Walter Clark occupied this shortly after arriving in Prescott in 1888. Dr. Clark sold this to the Water Commission, who sold it to the Eastern States Exposition in W. Springfield.

Atkinson Hollow Tavern

The Exposition remodeled this building, and added an ell to it. It is now part of the recreated New England village "Storrowtown" on the exposition grounds (off Rte. 147). A "tavern" restaurant is housed in the building.

Prescott Town Hall

When Prescott became a town in 1822, there was much controversy over where to locate the town hall. This was resolved in 1838 by the erection of this small building (and a cemetery) at the first road junction south of Atkinson Hollow.

The last town meeting was held in Prescott in March, 1928. It was voted to turn the town's functions over to the Water Commission, who ran it through appointed agents until its end in 1938.

Prescott Town Hall

The Water Commission sold this building to John M. Woolsey in 1930. Woolsey, a federal judge in New York, is best known for his decision allowing the controversial James Joyce novel *"Ulysses"* to be sold into the United States.

Woolsey, a summer resident of Petersham, had the building rebuilt on his property there, and called it his "country courthouse." While it is not open to the public, it is visible on a hilltop just north of St. Peter's Church on Rte. 32.

APPLICABLE REGULATIONS

The following regulations were applicable to the Quabbin Reservation when this book was printed. Any questions about them, or changes that may have been made since should be directed to the Visitor's Center at the Quabbin administration building. Their telephone number is 413-323-7221.

These regulations are excerpted from 350 CMR 11: 09 (2) (a) and (b). Regulations pertaining to shore and boat fishing have been omitted from this listing.

1. Entrance on and exit from land of the Watershed system shall be made through gates or other designated areas.
2. No person is allowed within any land of the Watershed System, except from one hour before sunrise to one hour after sunset, unless authorized by a written permit from the Commission.
4. All acts which pollute or may pollute the water supply are prohibited. No litter or refuse of any sort may be thrown or left in or on any land or water within any Watershed System. All persons shall use the sanitray facilities provided for public use.
5. All acts which injure the property of the Commonwealth are prohibited. No one shall injure, deface, destroy, remove, or carry off any property, real or personal, under the care and control of the Commission, including but not limited to all historic artifacts and natural materials.
6. Cooking and all fires are prohibited within the Watershed System.
7. & 8. No person shall swim or wade in any reservoir... (or) in any Tributatry or Surface Waters on or within the property of the Commonwealth.
9. Organized sports activities, including but not limited to orienteering and baseball, are prohibited in the Watershed System except by written permit from the Commission.
10. ....The Commission and its employees are not responsible... for any injury or loss of life which may be incurred in commection with public use of the reservoirs and Waershed System.

11. Breach of peace, profanity, or other disorderly conduct offensive to the general public is strictly prohibited... posession of and drinking of alcoholic beverages is prohibited within said System.

12. No person shall drive a motor vehicle within the Watershed System except upon roads authorized for such use by the Commission. Recreational vehicles are prohibited. Motor vehicles shall be parked only at areas designated by the Commission. No person shall willfully obstruct the free passage of vehicles or persons within the Watershed.

13. No person shall bring any animal within (the Quabbin Watershed).

14. The use of bicycles...shall be permitted only in areas designated by the Commission. (Currently only at Gates 29-30, 35, 40, and 43A-44 roads.)

18. Public assemblies of more than 25 persons shall not be allowed within the Watershed System without a permit from the Commission.

21. No person shall have posession of, or discharge any weapon, firearm, fireworks, or other explosive on or within the Watershed System.

22. No person may hunt, shoot, or trap animals on or within any Watershed System property except at times and in areas designated by the Commission.

23. All persons within the Watershed System shall obey the lawful directions of regulatory signs, police officers, persons in charge, or of Federal or Commonwealth wardens or enforcement officers.

24. The Watershed System or parts thereof may be closed for public access at the discretion of the Commission when necessary to protect the lands and waters.

25. The posession of all types of metal detectors or similar devices is prohibited on all of the Watershed System property.

SOURCES & FURTHER READING

(For more details on listings, see the author's *Bibliography of Quabbin Valley History*, 1992)

M.D.C. property plans, maps, files, and photos

Maps:

F. W. Beers' map atlases of Worcester (1870), Franklin (1871), & Hampshire (1873) Counties.
H. Walling 1857 wall maps of same counties
Scott & McLeran map of Hampshire County, 1854
L. Richards' Atlas of Worcester County, 1898
U. S. Geological Survey Topographic map sheets; Barre, Shutesbury, Winsor Dam, Quabbin Reservoir

Newspapers:

Amherst Record, Athol Transcript Athol Chronicle. Barre Gazette, Hampshire Gazette, Springfield Republican and Union

Books:

Bigelow, Paul: *Wrights & Privileges*, 1993
Clark, Walter; *Quabbin Reservoir*, 1946, repr.1994
Coolidge, Mabel C.: *History of Petersham,Ma.* 1948
Coolidge, L.P.: *Past Events of Prescott, Mass.*, 1949
Cox, Florence: *History of New Salem, Mass.*" 1953
Everts, L. (ed.): *History of the Connecticut River Valley*, 1879
Foye, William, *Trout Waters*, 1992
Greene, J.R.: *The Creation of Quabbin Reservoir*, 1981
Greene, J.R.: *An Atlas of the Quabbin Valley and the Ware River Diversion* 1989
Greene, J.R.: *The Day Four Quabbin Towns Died*, 1985
Greene, J.R.: *Strange Tales From Old Quabbin*, 1993
Gustafson, Evelina: *Ghost Towns 'Neath Quabbin Reservoir*, 1940
Howe, Donald (Compiler): *Quabbin: The Lost Valley*, 1951, reprinted 1992
Parmenter, C.: *History of Pelham, Mass.*, 1898
Russell, J.W.: *Vestiges of the Lost Valley: Buildings and Bells from the Quabbin* 1986